the good life

new public spaces for recreation

zoë ryan

with an essay
by Iain Borden

van alen institute
new york

AUG 14 2007

the fun city

the connected city

the healthy city

"But a state exists for the sake of a good life, and not for the sake of life only." (Steven Everson, ed., *Aristotle: The Politics*, Cambridge, UK: Cambridge University Press, 1988). So argued Aristotle and thereby set in motion the Western philosophical tradition of debate regarding the conditions of citizenship, the qualities of civic virtue, and the roles of these in what we have come to know as the public realm. Contemporary interpretations of the Greek *polis* have challenged Aristotle's founding arguments. Critical characterizations of the shape of modern polity set within global terms have contested ideal Enlightenment social models. And yet the project, as theorists such as Charles Taylor have described, of building the good life, the synthesis of public and private, endures as a core pursuit of the civil society enterprise.

New York has served as a staging ground for the project and for the pursuit. When in the 1850s Peter Cooper founded one of the first colleges to offer a free education to working-class young men and women and provided public reading rooms and meeting places for artists and inventors, he envisioned the revolutionary potentials of civic access. Long before such access became public policy, Frederick Law Olmsted submitted his "Greensward Plan" as a locus of democratic ideals to the Central Park Commission in the country's first landscape design contest. For Olmsted the public sphere had spatial or at least experiential implications and the most worthy expressions of democratic citizenship, he contended, were "not industry, nor well-balanced supply and demand nor sobriety and inoffensiveness" but rather "parks, gardens, music, dancing schools, reunions"—forms of public engagement and association that would support "unconscious, or indirect recreation." (Adam Gopnik, "Olmsted's Trip," *The New Yorker*, March 3, 1997).

Olmsted's desire to create a place and the opportunity for what he referred to as a common "gregariousness" has sustained urban civility throughout the city's history. It has unequivocally affirmed the power of public space. *The Good Life* exhibition organized by Van Alen Institute, pays tribute to the visionaries who have imagined such realms and presents the myriad ways in which the good life might be imagined anew. The exhibition, in so doing, continues Van Alen Institute's longstanding commitment to informing debate, across a broad range of discourses, related to the complex territories of public architecture, design, planning, and the public sphere.

We are grateful to Hudson River Park Trust for partnering on this project and allowing us to present the exhibition on Pier 40. In 1998 Van Alen Institute sponsored an open design competition for the pier as part of an initiative to study the New York waterfront. The interim years have witnessed the extraordinary renaissance of the West Side waterfront sites and the reclamation of the city's pastoral edge through the tremendous work and patronage of the Hudson River Park Trust. *The Good Life* exhibition brings us full circle in our efforts to celebrate inquiry, innovation, and provocation. On behalf of the trustees of Van Alen Institute, as well as its sponsors, partners, and members, we are honored to present the fantastic range of good life projects and look forward to our leadership and continued contributions to the field, defining new platforms for critical and dynamic civic engagement.

Adi Shamir
Executive Director
Van Alen Institute

acknowledgments

Major Sponsors
The Good Life exhibition—
National Endowment for the Arts
Graham Foundation for
    Advanced Studies in the Fine Arts
New York State Council on the Arts
Con Edison
Brightman Hill Charitable Foundation
Diane von Furstenberg
Josh Weisberg/Scharff Weisberg Inc.
Material for the Arts

Special thanks to
Hudson River Park Trust

The Good Life catalogue—
The Stephen A. and
    Diana L. Goldberg Foundation
Elise Jaffe + Jeffrey Brown

The planning for *The Good Life* began in fall 2004. Since then a diverse team of colleagues, friends, volunteers, and talented individuals have helped realize this project. On behalf of Van Alen Institute, I wish to thank the designers, architects, landscape architects, artists, their inspired clients, and the photographers whose work is featured in the exhibition and catalogue, for their cooperation, enthusiasm and generosity. I wish to also thank our sponsors (listed to the left) who made this exhibition and publication possible. I would like to thank Hudson River Park Trust, and in particular Connie Fishman, Noreen Doyle, Christopher Martin, David Katz, and Debra Kustka, for partnering with the Institute on this project and providing a stunning waterfront location on New York's Pier 40 for the exhibition.

I am indebted to the participants in the five roundtables held in 2005: Janet Abrams, Paola Antonelli, Benjamin Aranda, Diana Balmori, Donald Bates, Adrian Benepe, Michael Bierut, Andrew Darrell, Jonathan Evans, Carl Goodman, DeeDee Gordon, Jane Harrison, Mark Husser, Natalie Jeremijenko, Steven Johnson, Arnold Lehman, Jeanne Lutfy, Gregg Pasquarelli, Anne Pasternak, Charles Renfro, Susan T. Rodriguez, Katie Salen, Craig Schwitter, Kevin Slavin, Ken Smith, Cliff Sperber, Dana Spiegel, Paul Stoller, Marilyn Taylor, Marc Tsurumaki, Camille Utterback, Andrew C. Winters, and Dan Wood. Their comments and wisdom were essential during the research phase of the project. Many thanks to the esteemed video interviewees for their insights, in particular Robert Hammond and city officials Adrian Benepe, Amanda M. Burden, and David J. Burney. Thanks also to Iain Borden for his thoughtful essay that provides a guide to the most crucial elements in designing new public spaces for recreation.

Many thanks to the trustees of the Institute who contributed to the exhibition with their advice and support. In particular, I am deeply grateful to the exhibition committee: Adi Shamir, VAI's executive director; Sherida E. Paulsen, VAI's chair; and trustees Paola Antonelli and Susan T. Rodriguez, who believed strongly in this project and offered guidance and encouragement throughout. I would also like to thank Kadambari Baxi, Lisa Frigand, Richard Gluckman, Michael Manfredi, Craig Schwitter, Peter Slatin, and Marc Tsurumaki for their help and support.

Special thanks to the exhibition designers, Dan Wood and Amale Andraos from WORK Architecture Company, and Prem Krishnamurthy and Adam Michaels from Project Projects, for their steadfast belief in this project and continued enthusiasm, which ensured the creation of an inventive and inspiring exhibition design. Thanks also to Project Projects for creating this beautiful publication. I thank their design teams who worked tirelessly. From WORKac: Skye Beach, Olaf Haertel, Forrest Jessee, Anna Kenoff, Ryan Neiheiser, Dayoung Shin, and Linda Choe Vestergaard. For technical assistance, Scharff Weisberg Inc. For fabric consulting and design, Elastico, and in particular Elodie Blanchard. For construction consulting, Eze Bongo. From Project Projects: Caroline Askew, Chris McCaddon, and Ken Meier. Thanks to Local Projects for collaborating on the motion graphics, and to Craig Cook for video production. Thanks also to Eric Olson from Process Type Foundry and Fiona Gardner.

Special thanks to Frank Lantz and Kevin Slavin from area/code for developing an urban game that really got at the heart of *The Good Life* exhibition, and to their team: Erik Högstedt, Dennis Crowley, Michael Sharon, Dan Melinger, Wilson Chang, Kati London, Chris Paretti, and Scott Jon Siegel. Thanks also to Rob Faludi and Roger Abrahams. For providing an exceptional food and beverage service for the show, thanks to Florent Morellet and Restaurant Florent, especially Denise Dalfo, Harry Eriksen, and Michael Manhertz.

Many friends and colleagues sent ideas and gave precious advice and assistance. There are too many to name in full, but I would like to single out: Moji Baratloo, Kathy Battista, Kerstin Bergendal, Aaron Betsky, Henk Döll, Ana Maria Duran, Grant Gibson, Claudine Gumbel, Peter Schultz Jørgensen, Andrea Kahn, Daniel Kass, Jenny Kite, Cathy Lang Ho, Liane Lefaivre, Bart Lootsma, Stuart McDonald, Tracy Metz, Rowan Moore, Dan Nuxoll, Lene Roed Olesen, Vicky Richardson, Mark Elijah Rosenberg, Susan Solomon, Quentin Stevens, Deyan Sudjic, Alijd van Doorn, and Gavin Wade. A very special mention to Barış Bilen, and Brenda, Max, and Amy Ryan for their support throughout.

I would like to thank Princeton Architectural Press, especially Kevin Lippert and Clare Jacobsen, for their advice and for distributing this publication. Thanks also to Susan Grant Lewin Associates, especially Susan Grant Lewin, Michelle DiLello, Sarah Natkins, and Joan Goldberg for expertly handling the public relations for this project.

The staff at Van Alen Institute deserves special acknowledgment for their passionate support. For their dedication, I thank the VAI team, including Ori Topaz and Chun Ouyang who compiled the exhibition brochure of events throughout New York City, as well as Carolyn Acevedo, Ari Duraku, and Isaac H. Margulis. I wish also to thank former VAI staff members Jonathan Cohen-Litant and Marcus Woollen, as well as Katherine Meehan, Jason Rosen, and Karen Chin. Thanks also to Jonah Lowenfeld whose excellent copyediting made all the difference. I would like to give a special mention to curatorial assistant Elise Youn for her exceptional work, in particular writing many of the project descriptions for this catalogue. I would also like to especially acknowledge research assistant Karen Kice with whom I shared this journey and whose commitment, enthusiasm, and sterling work never wavered throughout the entirety of this project. Lastly, I wish to acknowledge former VAI Executive Director Raymond W. Gastil with whom the concept and title for *The Good Life* was conceived in 2004, and without whom this adventure would not have been possible.

Zoë Ryan
Senior Curator

please walk on the grass:
recreation and play in the contemporary city

zoë ryan

In our dense cities, recreational spaces are essential components of healthy and sustainable urban environments. Longer working hours, reduced vacation time, and growing health concerns are just some of the reasons why the need for public spaces in the centers of cities is increasingly important. The complex economic and political situation today has also intensified the need for such spaces that welcome and include citizens from diverse communities. But no matter one's background, how one's leisure time is spent in a city depends on the environment and facilities available. Recreational activities determine the quality of one's life. As Tracy Metz has noted, "Our social identity is determined by the way we spend our leisure at least as much as by the work we do or the possessions we own."[1]

Chosen for their innovative solutions and high-quality designs, the projects presented in *The Good Life: New Public Spaces For Recreation* explore how architects, designers, landscape architects, and artists are reinventing urban public spaces to meet the needs of 21st-century recreation. Whether an urban beach shipped in for the summer, a new public park on a formerly industrial waterfront, or a network of playgrounds, the seventy projects in this volume illustrate that providing getaway destinations near home and spaces for moments of relaxation and for group and individual activities is at the core of new urban planning and design initiatives worldwide. Ranging from designs for street corners and pocket parks to plans for entire districts, they collectively provide a cross-section of some of the most interesting new spaces for leisure around the world.

This volume is organized around five themes: *The Cultured City*, *The Connected City*, *The 24-Hour City*, *The Fun City*, and *The Healthy City*. These categories are not meant to be exhaustive and many of the projects incorporate more than one theme. They act as a framework for the projects and a means by which key issues, vital to contemporary discussions, can be explored.

The Cultured City
The central idea of *The Cultured City*—that culture is an essential component of urban development—emerged in America in the early 1980s. In 1983, for example, the Port Authority of New York and New Jersey published *The Arts as an Industry: Their Economic Importance to the New York-New Jersey Metropolitan Region*, a report that recognized the role of artists, creative industries, and cultural activities in the creation of a thriving city. In 1985, Europe also embraced this idea with the launch of the annual award for the European City of Culture, later renamed the European Capital of Culture. This European Union initiative enforced the notion that design, culture, and the arts are essential to urban development and regeneration.

Recent years have witnessed the publication of a number of seminal texts exploring the consequences of this development. In 2000, British theorist Charles Landry published *The Creative City:*

1 Tracy Metz, *FUN! Leisure and the Landscape* (Rotterdam, the Netherlands: NAI Publishers, 2002), 8.

2 Richard Florida, *The Rise of the Creative Class—And How It's Transforming Work, Leisure, Community and Everyday Life* (New York: Basic Books, 2002), 40.

A Toolkit for Urban Innovators. This volume outlines a history of the creative city and acts as a manual for creating a desirable urban environment by identifying and harnessing local resources, interests, and talents. In 2002, American theorist Richard Florida published *The Rise of the Creative Class—And How It's Transforming Work, Leisure, Community and Everyday Life*. Florida posits that a new, influential class of people has emerged who value creativity more than ever before and strive to cultivate it as part of their everyday lives. He writes that creative people are changing cities through their "desire for organizations and environments that let them be creative—that value their input, challenge them, have mechanisms for mobilizing resources around ideas, and are receptive to both small changes and the occasional big idea."[2] Florida's text is a call to arms for creative people to contribute to the common good. These texts, just two of the many written on this subject, are not without controversy, yet their message speaks to the idea of *The Cultured City* and the possibility for creativity to effect positive change on society and the built environment.

Projects in *The Cultured City* section draw references from across creative disciplines. The Idea Store in Whitechapel, London, is a new library concept that borrows concepts from the retail industry in an effort to create an accessible, eye-catching design that will engage local residents. Architect David Adjaye claims to be "deeply suspicious of a built environment which young people understand only in terms of shops and commerce," yet the success of the Idea Store, which expresses itself in those very same terms, has been overwhelming. "I have never seen, in anything that calls itself a library, that number of different kinds of people, in ethnic and gender terms," he notes.

Smaller-scale actions have also reawakened urban areas. London-based artists and architects Greyworld work on projects that they refer to as "transforming the grey areas of the city" by retooling standard elements of the cityscape, such as adding sounds and multiple functions to sidewalk railings and benches. San Francisco-based public artists and activists Rebar produce insightful public art projects that combine humor and activism, such as temporarily installing pocket parks in car parking spaces on city streets. Nimbus Design from Germany develops projects that the public can interact with, temporarily appropriating public space for themselves. For a project in Stuttgart, they installed oversized living-room lamps in the central square, the color of which could be changed by the public. These projects reinterpret the city as a stage on which novel ideas can be played out for public use. They illustrate that urban public spaces can have strong identities and engaging cultural programs that attract a broad public, ensuring vitality and relevance over time.

The 24-Hour City

24-hour cities are often considered the most desirable places to live, work, and play. Urban dwellers are prepared to tolerate the

3 Lewis Mumford, "The Culture of Cities," published in Philip Kasinitz, ed., *Metropolis: Center and Symbol of Our Times* (New York: New York University Press, 1995), 321.

inconveniences like noise, congestion, and high living costs in order to take advantage of the activities and entertainments that are available to them. As American historian Lewis Mumford argues, "By the diversity of its time-structures, the city in part escapes the tyranny of a single present, and the monotony of a future that consists In repeating only a single beat heard in the past. Through its complex orchestration of time and space, no less than through the social division of labor, life in the city takes on the character of a symphony: specialized human aptitudes, specialized instruments, give rise to sonorous results which, neither in volume nor in quality, could be achieved by any single piece."[3] Mumford's comments underline the advantages of the possibilities of 24-hour living in the city and the unique opportunities that this brings. *The 24-Hour City* projects embody Mumford's view of the urban environment in that they are flexible spaces that can accommodate different activities, whether programmed or spontaneous, and have the capacity to transform over time to encourage new uses, energizing the site at all times.

For the redesign of Lincoln Center for the Performing Arts in New York, for example, architecture firm Diller Scofidio + Renfro devised a scheme that would open up some of the buildings with new glass façades, unveiling the activity within. Making it possible to see dancers warming up or practicing at the New York City Ballet's studios will enliven the site day and night, whether or not performances are in session. Another project that adaptively reuses an existing structure is Flux Park in King's Cross, London, a new event destination being conceived by General Public Agency, an art, design, and architecture consultancy. The project takes a former gas tank and adapts it into a flexible environment with a 24-hour-a-day program of events and activities. Fostering cultural and social exchange is also at the heart of the transformation of the waterfront in Split, Croatia. This historical setting is the most important place of public life in the city. The redesign, led by Zagreb-based 3LHD Architects, aims to open up the waterfront promenade with a variety of spaces that can better cater to the growing numbers of events—social gatherings, sport events, religious festivals, processions, political demonstrations, markets—taking place there.

The 24-Hour City projects focus primarily on making public spaces that are accessible, fostering community engagement and active participation in urban life. They demand diversity of all kinds: juxtapositions of people, functions, built forms, spaces, and activities are just some of the fundamental elements that help encourage an inclusive and sustainable public sphere that thrives day and night.

The Fun City

At the core of *The Fun City* is the notion of play, famously explored in the 1930s by Dutch historian Johan Huizinga. He writes that play is a "voluntary activity or occupation executed within certain fixed limits

4 Johan Huizinga, *Homo Ludens* (English translation; New York: Roy Publishers, 1950), 28.

5 Roger Caillois, *Man, Play and Games* (English translation; Chicago: University of Illinois Press, 2001), 9-10.

6 Susan G. Solomon, *Recent American Playgrounds: Revitalizing Community Space* (Hanover, NH and London: University Press of New England, 2005), 1.

7 Liane Lefaivre, Henk Döll, and Alijd van Doorn, *Ground Up City: Play as a Design Tool* (Rotterdam: Döll-Atelier voor Bouwkunst, 2005), 5.

8 Ibid.

of time and place, according to rules freely accepted but absolutely binding, having its aim in itself and accompanied by a feeling of tension, joy, and consciousness that it is different from ordinary life."[4] Twenty years later, French theorist Roger Caillois instead defined play as an activity which is essentially free, separate, uncertain, unproductive, governed by rules, and make-believe.[5]

What binds their differing opinions is the importance they place on play as a part of everyday life. Although play is proven to be beneficial to the physical and mental development of both children and adults, increased demands on our time, heightened security and safety concerns in public spaces, and the growing amount of structured activity that dominates our daily lives are having adverse effects on play spaces in cities globally. Susan Solomon, an expert on children's playgrounds writes that they "used to reflect theories about how children learn; today they are largely unconnected to seasoned beliefs on the subject...The playground has become so safe that it no longer allows children to take on challenges that will further educational and emotional development."[6] Her sentiment is confirmed by Adrian Benepe, the commissioner of New York City's Department of Parks and Recreation, in his comments published in this volume. "Our state legislature," he explains, "force[s] us to be nannies and build these really boring and safe places where there is no risk at all."

In 2005, Dutch art historian Liane Lefaivre completed a study that investigated how play might be reincorporated as part of urban planning and design processes for inner-city communities. Through her research, undertaken in collaboration with Henk Döll and Alijd van Doorn from the Rotterdam-based firm Döll-Atelier voor Bouwkunst, she determined that playgrounds in cities are essential meeting places for people of different ages and backgrounds.[7] Her study explores the importance of play spaces for children and adults, starting from historical examples such as Aldo van Eyck's playgrounds designed in the Netherlands to the contemporary fitness equipment she found on the streets of Shanghai and Beijing. (While in Istanbul recently, this author also came across exercise and play equipment in public parks used by people of all ages.) Lefaivre uses these examples to show how play is a necessary component of the urban environment and should be considered "as a design theme" within new city architecture.[8]

Included in *The Fun City* projects is a planned playscape on top of a department store in the center of Copenhagen, a unique recreational space like none other in the city. This accessible venue is intended to generate new types of activities and interactions currently missing from daily life. A new skateboard park in San Juan, Puerto Rico, aims to integrate skaters and non-skaters in a recreational venue that both can enjoy—a tough task, but one that designer and artist Vito Acconci hopes can be achieved through a design that functions as a performance space with designated areas for spectators.

9 Jane Jacobs, *The Death and Life of Great American Cities* (New York: Vintage Books, 1992), 29.

In Japan, Takano Landscape Planning Company's parks in Tachikawa and Obihiro City might have been intended for children, but their diversity of play spaces, ranging from huge bouncy domes to artificial fog forests, have proved to be hits with all ages, encouraging cross-generational exploration and interaction. These designs provide novelty, unpredictability, and surprise in the urban environment, but also promote social cohesion.

The Connected City

Since the end of World War II, the battle between cars and the city has figured increasingly in city politics and urban planning. In *The Highway and the City*, published in 1963, Lewis Mumford foresaw "a tomb of concrete roads and ramps covering the dead corpse of the city." The future has not proved to be quite so dismal, yet the mass of traffic in urban centers has triggered radical responses. These include Mayor Ken Livingstone's congestion charge in London that came into effect in 2003. The $13-per-day-fee has reportedly reduced traffic by 18 percent and generated revenue for upgrading public transportation, prompting discussions of similar initiatives globally.

And yet the city's streets are about more than just the movement of vehicles and people. The late American urban theorist Jane Jacobs asserted that the "Streets and their sidewalks, the main public places of a city, are its most vital organs...If a city's streets look interesting, the city looks interesting; if they look dull, the city looks dull."[9]

The Connected City projects show how designers and architects are creating networks of urban public spaces and rethinking the routes between them. For example, the High Line, an abandoned elevated railroad in New York, is being transformed into a new urban park. This public project will provide much-needed green space as well as link three neighborhoods along the West Side of Manhattan. Robert Hammond, director of Friends of the High Line, the non-profit organization spearheading the project, points out that people will be able to cross more than 20 city blocks without ever encountering a car or truck. "It will be a truly unique urban experience." He hopes that the project will "create a connection that will revitalize these neighborhoods by increasing pedestrian traffic and thus creating an economic boost." Metropolitan Park in Rio de Janeiro is intended to foster connections between people and places in an area where tensions run high between the informal favela communities and the surrounding neighborhoods of the city. Architect Jorge Mario Jáuregui says that Rio has been "strongly marked by the inequalities generated by development processes that are based on quantity and private benefits rather than quality and social benefits," and his plan is that the park will create a democratic space for use by all and be a "gesture of confidence" in the city.

The Connected City is also linked by a complex network of virtual spaces, accessed by wireless communications and new

10 James Wines, *Green Architecture* (Cologne, Germany: Taschen, 2000), 20.

11 Ibid., 19.

technologies. As Marshall McLuhan foresaw in *The Medium is the Massage: An Inventory of Effects*, in 1967, electronic media has brought about the return of a collective way of perceiving the world. What he could not have predicted was the possibility for individualizing experience via new technology in public space. Dana Spiegel, executive director of NYCwireless, a non-profit organization that advocates and enables the growth of free, public wireless internet access in New York City, explains that "by providing hotspots or wireless internet portals at sites throughout the city, residents and visitors can access information about local events and businesses as well as add personal comments or useful facts for future users." This project exemplifies how the internet has made possible access to localized information about any public place, anywhere, anytime.

The *Connected City* projects include ATOPIA's new media and communication system for an area the size of an urban district. The team's Battersea Power Station project in London is, in their words, "a major opportunity to imagine, design, and ultimately implement a new kind of public space using the most advanced communications technology in a unique commercial context." Visitors to the mixed-use, 36-acre site will be able to download information about events and activities at the arts institutions in the complex to their PDAs and other wireless communications devices as they enter. The effect will be an immersive technological environment. The diverse projects in this section, whether physical or virtual, show that the exchange of ideas and information is a fundamental part of *The Connected City*, encouraging movement and exploration that animates and informs the urban environment.

The Healthy City

The 21st century has so far been characterized by increased threats to our planet's environment and biodiversity. In 2000, James Wines asserted that the challenge facing architects is the integration of "environmental technology, resource conservation, and aesthetic content," into the design of the built environment.[10] He writes that the first decade of the 21st century could be labeled the "Age of Ecology."[11]

One of the most important initiatives in urban places worldwide is the integration of more parks and green spaces with trees and plants that can dampen noise levels, filter pollution, absorb carbon dioxide and produce oxygen, absorb rainwater and reduce run-off, and provide shade. These spaces also encourage physical activity, and may help address worrisome health issues such as the rising level of child obesity. In New York City, for example, a three-pronged scheme is being introduced that will integrate more greenways, bike paths, and playgrounds into the dense urban fabric.

As the projects in *The Healthy City* section illustrate, visionary thinking at both small and large scales can have dramatic impacts on our cities. The potential for formerly industrial sites to be

12 Michael Walzer, "Pleasures and Costs of Urbanity," published in Philip Kasinitz, ed., *Metropolis: Center and Symbol of Our Times* (New York: New York University Press, 1995), 321.

13 Ibid.

transformed into new public spaces for recreation and leisure is being discovered globally. In Santa Fe, New Mexico, a former railyard is being reconceived as a public park in the heart of the downtown area. In Malmö, Sweden a former car factory has been turned into a waterfront park. In Seattle, Washington, extensive remediation has enabled a former brownfield site on the waterfront to be converted into a sculpture park. Concepts for healthier options than traveling by car in cities have the potential for widespread influence on future city planning and urban design processes. In Manchester and Toronto, designers are working on ideas for new recreational highways that encourage biking, jogging, and even swimming as alternative methods of commuting into the city. These projects underscore that for *The Healthy City* to succeed, designs need to focus on environmental and ecological sustainability but also on political, economic, educational, and cultural sustainability.

This brief exploration of the major themes in this volume demonstrates that the best and most sustainable public spaces engage a broad range of users, are designed for both large- and small-scale interventions and events, and are flexible to change over time, accommodating multiple activities, both programmed and unscripted. Good design serves both individual and collective needs. These innovative new public spaces are highlighted for their ability to be appropriated by people from diverse communities, for encouraging multiple experiences, and for fostering social and cultural exchange. Projects like these prompt discovery, help promote understanding and tolerance, and enhance the quality of our everyday lives.

The projects have one thing in common; they are all "open-minded space," to borrow Michael Walzer's term. He maintains that citizens in a city that is designed for a variety of uses and people, including the unexpected and the predictable, "do different things and are prepared to tolerate, even take an interest in, things they don't do."[12] It is the design of the city and its public spaces that enables this open-mindedness to emerge, stimulating individual and group expression and encouraging engaged citizenship. Walzer further argues, "It's not only that space serves certain purposes known in advance by its users, but also that its design and character stimulate (or repress) certain qualities of attention, interest, forbearance, and receptivity. We act differently…because of what it means to be 'there,' and because of the look and feel of the space itself."[13]

Well-designed urban public spaces should aim to address the needs of city dwellers to rebalance their lives, offering a refuge from the hustle and bustle or a place in which they can develop through learning and new experiences. People need to connect with their environment and feel a sense of belonging, to feel good being there—therein lies the good life.

the cultured city

We live in an age in which the quality of the public realm is driven by the ability of our streets, open spaces, parks, plazas, commercial and cultural centers to tell us stories and give meaning to life. As American social theorist Richard Florida has noted, cities are increasingly being valued for the level of creativity that they inspire and encourage. In the current political, economic, and social climate, it is important that cities have strong identities and engaging programs that are accessible to a broad range of cultures and economic groups. Access to the arts, education, culture, and design is an integral element of the fabric of the urban environment promoting diversity, education, creativity, tolerance, and the exchange of ideas.

The following projects illustrate how cities across the world are fostering activities that encourage social interaction and skill-building. In less privileged communities in London, Soweto, and the Serbian city of Novi Sad, new public recreational and cultural centers are reinventing traditional spaces for learning, playing, and socializing. In New York and Milan, new parks are providing access to nature and are creating opportunities for cultural and environmental education through diverse landscape conditions and facilities for adults and children. In Rotterdam, a new park is being designed for local residents focused on community activities and hobbies as part of a larger renewal project for a depressed urban area. In Denia, Spain, an elevated artificial landscape forged into the natural surroundings has given the city a dynamic town square activated by a theater, a museum, and an open-air amphitheater. In addition to large-scale initiatives, a diverse collection of smaller-scale interventions from public art and urban games, to installations and performances, illustrate the importance and potential of more grassroots methods of investigating how we use, understand, play in, construct, and cultivate the city. *The Cultured City* projects illustrate that the best and most sustainable public spaces are those that are flexible to change and can accommodate multiple activities, both programmed and unscripted. —ZR

roundtable discussion

jonathan evans
managing director,
ralph appelbaum associates

carl goodman
deputy director & director of digital media,
museum of the moving image

mark husser
principal, grimshaw, new york

arnold lehman
director, brooklyn museum of art

jeanne lutfy
president, brooklyn academy of music
local development corporation

susan t. rodriguez
partner, polshek partnership and VAI trustee

camille utterback
artist in the field of interactive installation

*The following conversation took place in
spring 2005 at Van Alen Institute. This text is
an edited version of the original transcript.*

evans There are some significant contradictions
faced by our institutions and museums related
to the use of technology. One is that technology
has allowed us to customize experience. With web-
based technologies, for example, everybody feels
entitled to have their own experience of a museum.
I think what is really important about education in
a museum setting that sometimes gets lost is for
an institution to present its point of view and values
while allowing for practices that encourage people
to follow their own investigations.

goodman Much of the interactive technology
used in museums as interpretive programming
makes people feel as though they are involved or
have something to say but in fact controls what
they can do.

utterback I have been working on projects that
create spaces in which people can test their
own assumptions. For example, I did a piece for
the American Museum of Natural History in
New York as part of "The Genomic Revolution"
show in 2001. A live video of visitors was projected
on the gallery wall. Instead of displaying normal
video, my piece translated people's images
into the letters ATGC, which represent the
proteins of DNA. I hoped that after the initial fun
of seeing themselves that people would start
asking, is that me? Do those letters represent me?
This question was raised throughout the exhibit,
but my piece allowed people to encounter it in
a very personal and subjective way.

goodman This technique of putting a mirror in
front of museum visitors and asking them to look at
themselves is a dramatic gesture that is itself not
educational, but opens the door for education and
visitor involvement, which is vital for learning.

lehman The most successful education program
that we have had recently was a complete surprise
to us. It was for the "Great Expectations: John
Singer Sargent Painting Children" exhibition.
We invited children to sit for a portrait. Visitors went
through the exhibition reading about Sargent's
various sitters and looking at his portraits and at

the end of the show had the opportunity to have their photograph taken. Over 10,000 people sat for portraits. We lined a gallery from floor to ceiling with these images and comments. The photographers commented on how many times the sitters would go back and forth into the gallery in order to be able to mimic a formal seating arrangement Sargent had established. The exhibition became very interactive.

evans Technology allows us to think that every-thing can be customized and people can have an at-home experience that duplicates a museum experience or an art experience or a cultural experience. At the same time, people miss being in a space in which they can have a communal experience. I think a current concern is how do you honor those kinds of impulses—the individualization of experience and the real need for people to be in public spaces together?

lutfy One of the things that we realized when we were developing the master plan for BAM Cultural District with Rem Koolhaas and Diller Scofidio + Renfro is that we wanted to encourage interaction between people and artists, as well as between art organizations from various disciplines. We wanted to design the district's landscape so that it would foster connections between the Cultural District and the surrounding communities. We also wanted to design and program the public spaces to make the district an inviting destination that people would want to come to hang out in, pass through, or enjoy the arts and activities going on. As we move forward with the project, we plan to literally incorporate artists' works into the landscape. We will use design and architecture as tools to elevate the level of awareness about the district's surroundings and the cultural diversity that is inherent in these spaces.

rodriguez I think that in order to create a healthy and sustainable city in a broader sense you need to provide places that are accessible to all. The city is inherently a percolator of information but one of our major concerns as designers, educators, cura-tors, etc., is how do you draw different people in?

utterback I think the question of accessibility is essential to discussions about education and the arts. My work is always about transforming the public's experience of a place or a situation, allowing them to reflect on it, and through that encouraging them to engage in more didactic information. The message does not need to be overt but can be more subliminal and still have an impact. It is about sparking people's curiosity first and then working on holding people's attention long enough so that they explore the work, whether that's an art piece or a public space.

lehman At the Brooklyn Museum of Art, we just opened the door. I had wondered for many, many years how to engage the hundreds, if not thousands of schoolchildren who walked by our museum but never looked or came in. By creating more access points and a more transparent entrance, designed by Polshek Partnership, these kids now walk through the museum. In addition, one of the reasons that we still have a suggested admission rather than a fixed admission fee is exactly for these kids. If by chance one of them decides not just to walk in and see what is hanging in the lobby but maybe wants to see an exhibit they do not have to think twice and say "But it is going to cost me $5 or $20?" They can just walk in.

rodriguez I went recently to the Seattle Public Library, designed by Rem Koolhaas and the Office for Metropolitan Architecture. It is a stunning space, but what stuck in my mind, which I still can't get over, is that you can drink a cup of coffee in the library. You can in fact bring your coffee into any part of the library. In one sense it changes the library from a place in which you study, to a place of recreation. It is a simple idea but it totally changes your perception of what the space is used for and makes the concept of the library much less formal and more accessible.

goodman At the Museum of the Moving Image, we have been investigating how people access information. Our interest in handheld devices emerged out of seeing visitors who come to the museum with some form of electronic device in their pocket: a cell phone, a media player, or a PDA. We wanted to take advantage of this and create a way for people to utilize their personal device to access information about the exhibitions and events within the context of the museum. The idea was to enhance the intimate relationship visitors have with their digital devices and find a way to enter into this relationship rather than compete with it.

Though this technology can distance people from their surrounding physical environment, experiences can be designed that aid social interaction. For instance, people can share the information they have on their personal devices with one another.

rodriguez One of the things I'm curious about is how technology is transforming how we design and think about our physical, personal, and collective spaces. How important is the physical place to conveying information? Can technology be used to go beyond the walls of an institution or a specific neighborhood?

goodman What we are interested in is exploring how we can connect a visit to a museum with the visit of that same person to our website. We want people to be able to bookmark a physical object within the museum, and access that information later via a personal point of entry on our website.

lehman We've developed a PDA system called Pocket Museum, which gives visitors access to everything in our collection database.

lutfy Is it connected to the website?

lehman Yes, visitors can get onto the museum's website through the PDA. Unfortunately, they can also just sit in a chair in the lobby and go through the entire museum, but hopefully, they will explore exhibits, and as they go through, they can access information which will encourage them to explore further.

lutfy Again, I think that what is important about all these projects that are being mentioned is the idea of connectivity. With the BAM Cultural District, we want the district not only to be about the presentation of art, but also about its creation, so spaces need to be able to accommodate both. Our plan is to develop a sense of transparency between the buildings and public spaces so that people can see what's going on, get engaged, and make connections between difference spaces.

rodriguez Your point about connections is critical when thinking about the cultured city. In designing the new Frank Sinatra High School for the Arts in Astoria, Queens, we've created a large glass curtain wall facing the Museum of the Moving Image and Kaufman Studios, in order to enliven the avenue with the arts program within the building. The glass façade will become a luminous beacon at night when the school's concert hall is open to the public.

goodman Schouwburgplein in Rotterdam, designed by West 8, is very interesting in this regard. The square has a series of light posts that the public can play around with by changing their position. It can be off-putting at first but then it is actually quite wonderful.

evans Education is not just about making cerebral connections or connections through technology, but is also about personal engagements that affect all of the senses. It is about something as simple as being able to walk down the street and have a conversation and casual encounter with things and people. For me, urban environments are all about trying to reinforce the collective memory of a city and build on that through the everyday experiences and encounters that are both programmed and unscripted.

lutfy A key ingredient for a public project such as the BAM Cultural District to succeed is ensuring that there is a demand for what you are doing. There needs to be a critical mass of people that embrace the idea. One of the great things happening in New York right now is the dispersal of arts organizations, artists, and the general population from Manhattan to the other boroughs. As a result, there is a critical mass of people that either needs or wants to participate in a project such as the Cultural District. That demand is enabling projects such as ours to take root.

rodriguez It takes leadership to make that happen and a commitment by the city.

husser I think it would be fascinating to explore how we might experience a museum environment or new ways of connecting with information at an urban scale. While recently waiting on jury duty downtown, I received this pamphlet about Lower Manhattan listing all of the significant downtown sites and their histories. It was fascinating. There was so much great information in there that I never would have found myself, yet because it was made available to me, I learned a lot.

goodman I am a big fan of a company called Sound Walks. They produce audio-based walking tours of New York City neighborhoods such as Times Square, the Bronx, Chinatown, Dumbo, and Williamsburg. Not just a voice droning on and on, they provide an audio soundscape that more closely connects you with the site's history and perhaps its essence. These are examples of projects that really add something to our experience and knowledge of public space.

Idea Store Whitechapel

Adjaye/Associates   London, United Kingdom   2005

The Idea Store in the Borough of Tower Hamlets, East London, is an ambitious attempt to reinvent the traditional neighborhood library. The project was conceived in 2000 to encourage lifelong learning, raise standards in literacy and numeracy, and foster healthy living among the borough's ethnically and culturally diverse population of around 200,000, as well as to stimulate urban regeneration of the local area. In 2005, the third Idea Store was completed in Whitechapel. The project was designed by Tanzanian-born, London-based David Adjaye, one of Britain's leading contemporary architects. Since opening, attendance has been approximately 54,500 visits per month compared with 14,600 visits in former library facilities in London. Open seven days a week, until 9 pm on some nights, the 50,000-square-foot Idea Store has a lending library that includes books, videos, and CDs, a café, exhibition space, classrooms, recreational spaces, and an IT center.

Adjaye is interested in rethinking social space in the urban environment. He explains that the Idea Store reinterprets the 19th-century model of the public institution, which "has reached the end of its shelf life," as an intuitive response to the contemporary context. The resulting five-story structure, wrapped in a multi-colored ribbon of clear, green, and blue glass alternating with glass-faced aluminum panels, references the striped roofs of the nearby market stalls, yet stands out against the gritty urban context of Whitechapel Road.

The overall theme of the building is openness and accessibility. While the glass and aluminum curtain wall creates visual connections between the action on the street and the activities within the building, skylights allow daylight to enter the building from above. Automatic doors at the entrance of the library and a giant escalator taking visitors directly to the class-rooms and workshops on the upper levels further encourage public access. Heather Wills, Idea Store Project Director for the Tower Hamlets Borough Council affirms that the building "is fast becoming the focal point for the local community, a place where people can go to relax, socialize, and learn in

a wholly integrated environment where there is something for everyone."

The concept for the Idea Stores is borrowed from the retail industry. Yet their highly trafficked locations and brand name focus on improving access to education, the arts, and culture rather than commercial activity. Adjaye has created a bold design that animates

the local context, suggesting positive change and an optimistic future for the people it serves. —ZR

1 North façade of
Idea Store, White-
chapel, London
2 Idea Store, with
Whitechapel Market
in foreground
3 Idea Store on
Whitechapel Road
4, 5 Interior views
of Idea Store

Denia Mountain Project

Guallart Architects   Denia, Spain   2010

In the city of Denia, along the Mediterranean coast of Spain, a new cultural park built over the site of a former quarry is the linchpin in a larger initiative to create a sustainable development in the city's historic center. Subject to haphazard development as tourists buy and build homes along the coast, Denia currently experiences an annual population increase from 40,000 in the winter to 150,000 in the summer. The site of the new cultural park is in the center of the city. The quarry is located on one side of a hill, while on the other side sits a castle dating from 100 BC. In 2002, Spanish architect Vicente Guallart won a national competition led by the city to transform the site into a new architectural landmark that will act as a major cultural, tourist and economic attraction.

Guallart approached the $40 million project with the premise that, "if architecture is landscape, then buildings are mountains." His design called for an artificial hillside to be built over the quarry to extend the city's public space and provide cultural, civic, and social amenities. Although pathways traverse the hill, Guallart's design makes new use of a tunnel dug into the hillside during the Spanish Civil War, creating a direct route from the city center to the park.

The principal part of the project is the multi-use center that will be built over the quarry, restoring the north face of the hillside. Guallart explains that his goal was to "create an artificial topography understood not as a skin, but as a genetic expression of the structure of the original stone of the quarry." Inspired by the angular forms of the limestone and the rhombohedric calcite crystals that make up the structural system for the hill, Guallart Architects set out to create a new design that borrowed similar geometric forms to create not only an artificial landscape over the existing hill but also the programmatic elements. "In this way," explains Guallart, "the skin of the buildings, like the soil, directly reflects the internal logic of the hill." For example, the cultural center's asymmetrical design resembles a rock formation and is seamlessly integrated into the structure of the hill.

The center will have three programmed areas: an exhibition space and auditorium for cultural events and the like; a public square known as the Agora, which will be open 24 hours a day and activated by a commercial zone of shops, restaurants, bars, and a cinema, as well as a spa, which is adjacent to a saltwater lake. Guallart Architects' integrated approach to designing this complex, multi-functional space focuses on how to increase urban development while protecting and nurturing the existing environment. The result is a contemporary cultural center and recreational space that references its historical setting. —ZR

1 Aerial view of Denia Mountain, Denia, Spain 2 Denia Mountain 3 Entrance to cultural park 4 Entrance to outdoor auditorium

SOMOHO

Mandla Mentoor and Katy Marks   Soweto, South Africa   2002

In the Johannesburg township of Soweto, the area of Tshiawelo was known for crime, garbage, and squatters for decades until the local community decided to take action and reclaim the land for public use. During the apartheid era, community leader Mandla Mentoor spearheaded a clean-up operation and recycling program throughout the city. Under his direction, local youth groups collected waste and used it to make papier-mâché art. The project proved so successful that an organization was founded in 1990 called Amandla Waste Creations. A decade later and in need of a larger space for their operations, Mentoor turned to the Tshiawelo hillside as a site for his environmental and cultural initiatives. He explains that "the first step in reclaiming this space was simply to be there and for people to show that they were not afraid to be there. The group was skilled in papier-mâché and sculpture so they distributed sculptures all over the site." Mentoor tapped into the interests and

skills of the community, inviting them to appropriate the space for their own needs. The hill was gradually cleared and equipment was set up for cooking, listening to music, and performing. Makeshift structures were made from found materials such as bags of earth, wood, rubber tires, and glass bottles. With help from the local people, the "brief for what should happen to the hill developed gradually with real needs, interests, and organizational structures," says Mentoor.

The focal point of the project is the adaptive reuse of the water tower at the summit of the hill. Funding from the British High Commission, the Canadian Government, and the Development Bank of Southern Africa enabled Mentoor to commission British architect Katy Marks, whose work focuses on sustainable development, to establish a low-cost solution to transform the water tower into a community center. Marks worked on stabilizing the structure and designed a staircase to provide access, along with a series of

structural shutters. Local school groups worked with her to produce metalwork and murals that decorate the exterior of the tower. Completed in 2002, the tower is now used for community workshops, dance and weaving classes, and has a stage for performances. Marks asserts that the project has created "both a literal and metaphorical common ground in an environment still burdened with violence and poverty."

With a growing membership of 300 local people, SOMOHO (Soweto Mountain of Hope) continues to evolve and change depending on the needs of the community. In September 2002, a group of world leaders led by UN Secretary General Kofi Annan visited the site as part of the World Summit on Sustainable Development. The project sets a precedent for bringing people together in a fun and active way to transform a neighborhood from the inside out. —ZR

1 SOMOHO, Soweto,   2 Drumming workshop
South Africa   3 Weaving workshop

1

Stadium Culture

Srdjan Jovanovic Weiss/NAO   Novi Sad, Serbia   2007

The near-decade-long civil war in the former Yugoslavia in the 1990s has left countries such as Serbia in a state of flux. As its cities emerge from this crisis and consider urban regeneration schemes, the focus has turned to the importance of creating new public spaces, cultural institutions, and recreational spaces for young people which can encourage social integration and exchange. Srdjan Jovanovic Weiss, a New York-based, Serbian-born architect is currently researching self-organization and micro-politics in the former Yugoslavia. He has been documenting the growing number of abandoned recreational spaces throughout Novi Sad, Serbia's second-largest city, located one hour north of Belgrade. In 2001, he partnered with kuda.org, a non-profit new media and communications group founded in the 1990s. Together, they proposed a project that would adapt an existing handball stadium located in the oldest part of Novi Sad

into a hybrid center for sports and electronic media culture. Jovanovic Weiss calls it "a locus for recreation, creativity, and exchange in a city without institutions for young people, and as a counter to the current political focus on nationalist regimes."

The design maximizes the use of the handball stadium for recreational activities by cantilevering a media center and viewing platform above concrete bleachers. The 8,500-

square-foot elevated structure will house an electronic info-lounge, rooms for workshops and presentations, offices, audio-visual studios, a café, and a store. A roof terrace on the top of the building is envisioned as an event space. —ZR

1 Stadium Culture, Novi Sad, Serbia

Eib's Pond Park Classroom

Marpillero Pollak Architects   Staten Island, New York   2000

Since 1998, Marpillero Pollak Architects (MPA), led by Sandro Marpillero and Linda Pollak, has been working with various local and citywide groups on the Eib's Pond Park Open Space Restoration and Recreation Project to create a 17-acre wetland park for use by the general public in Staten Island, one of New York City's five boroughs. The seeds of this project were planted in 1997 when the non-profit group New Yorkers for Parks (NY4P), together with a local tenants association and school conducted a study to determine how

to make the freshwater wetland at Eib's Pond accessible for public use. The resulting "Design Guidelines for a Wetland Park" recommended that small-scale measures such as the construction of an outdoor classroom for use by the community would help strengthen access to the wetlands and its ecological reserve.

In spring 1998, MPA was invited by NY4P to prepare a strategic plan for the park. In 1999, they designed the classroom to be accessed by a bridge, which was installed the following year with a $25,000 grant from NY4P and

help from Americorps workers. Pollak says that, "The objective was to use architecture to jumpstart a process, as a demonstration, allowing people to perceive that something could happen at their park while longer-term development was going on."

The 320-square-foot classroom can accommodate thirty. The frame of the open structure, which overlooks Eib's Pond and provides views across the wetland, is made from redwood and clad in weather- and damage-resistant recycled plastic lumber. The sheltered classroom has built-in benches around its edges and a central table with openings in its surface to display pond samples for study. A pier extending from the classroom provides immediate access to the pond. MPA's self-stated goal "was to transform what was once the 'backyard' of Staten Island into a valued 'front yard' and encourage investigations into the civic role of natural spaces within the urban environment." —ZR

1, 2 Eib's Pond Classroom, Staten Island, New York

Biblioteca degli Alberi

Inside Outside Team   Milan, Italy   2009

In 2004, the Netherlands-based multidisciplinary design firm, Inside Outside, working with an international group of collaborators, won an invited competition to design a new 25-acre public park on a wasteland site in Milan. The design called for botanical gardens, wooded areas, orchards, water features, and a series of public plazas. It is the first part of an $84 million redevelopment of the area to the north of the historic center of Milan, which has been left predominantly undeveloped since World War II. The project, driven by Milan's City Council, calls for 250,000 square feet of new buildings that will help transform this urban area into a cultural destination. In addition to commercial buildings, housing, and restaurants, it will include shops, a market, a university, a museum dedicated to fashion and design, art galleries, a community center, a sports center, and a museum of flowers and insects.

Petra Blaisse of Inside Outside built an interdisciplinary design team to work on the project that included Michael Maltzan Architecture, urban designer Mirko Zardini, landscape engineering firm RoD'or, graphic designer Irma Boom, and horticulturalist Piet Oudolf. Their first gesture was to rename the project to differentiate their design from more traditional parks in Milan. The design team selected "Biblioteca degli Alberi" (Library of Trees) to illustrate their overarching theme for the park, a series of "botanical libraries," rich with a diverse range of plants, grasses, trees, and flowers. "We designed a botanical library with a multitude of different gardens and spaces that play a major role in energizing the park," says Blaisse.

The main feature of the design is a complex system of pathways and bridges that crisscross the park and establish connections not only to major roads in the city, but also to gardens, open spaces, and event areas. Visitors are continually reminded of the urban setting yet are surrounded by an intense area of wildlife and greenery. The pathways house the main infrastructure for the park, including drainage, electricity,

irrigation, and lighting. They also function as an informational system: each route is embedded with text that identifies and gives the history of the nearby plants and trees. Each pathway will have its own identity through the use of materials and functions such as walking, reading, cycling, or sunbathing. The areas in between have been divided into five main zones: the lawn, the prairie, the shrubbery, water features, and hard surfaces including playgrounds, event spaces, and parking. These areas will be interspersed with circular groves of trees and orchards growing apples and almonds that provide high points of visual interest and color above the landscape. This new urban park systematically ties together a mass of heterogeneous elements and in doing so defies former park designs by creating a complex network of spaces and zones of activity for all to enjoy. —ZR

1 Plan of Biblioteca degli Alberi, Milan, Italy   2 Detail of Biblioteca degli Alberi 3 Aerial view

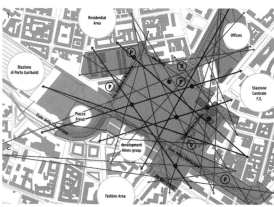

Heerlijkheid Hoogvliet   FAT   Hoogvliet, the Netherlands   2007

Hoogvliet, located five miles from the center of Rotterdam, was built in the 1940s as a new town that would serve the city's rapidly expanding population of workers required by the port. The former medieval village of Hoogvliet was replaced with a new town lined with towers and large apartment buildings. Shops, schools, public spaces, and transportation networks were also developed.

The addition of a new highway and subway line to Rotterdam resulted in the rapid decline of Hoogvliet's local amenities, engendering a feeling of alienation. Today, the town of 37,000 is marked by a desolate town square and has a reputation for crime and drug dealing. In the mid-1990s, it was proclaimed a disaster zone by the local authorities and a clean-up operation was initiated. The local authorities and the two private housing corporations that own most of Hoogvliet's housing stock came together to cooperate on a new vision for the area, and in 1999, the "Wimby!: Welcome into My Backyard!" project was born. Led by Felix Rottenberg, former chairman of the PvdA, a Dutch social-democratic political party, and two architectural historians, Michelle Provoost and Wouter Vanstiphout, their goal was to introduce an urban revitalization scheme based on a four-pronged approach to address social, economic, architectural, and urban issues.

They initiated a series of discussion groups and workshops to engage local residents in thinking about their town, which proved immensely popular. The resulting ideas inform the master plan for Hoogvliet, developed by Maxwan Architects and Planners.

One result of this collaborative initiative is the Heerlijkheid Hoogvliet, a new community park designed by London-based architecture office FAT (Fashion, Architecture, Taste). The 13-acre park, set to open in fall 2007, is situated to the north of the town in a green zone between the town and the highway. The design is a response to the personal desires of local residents who took part in a series of workshops which determined the program for the site. The park has event spaces, an open-air cinema, a lake, sports facilities, picnic areas with barbecues, and

a pet cemetery. The park also features "hobby huts," spaces that can be rented inexpensively by members of the community as workshop and studio spaces. Sam Jacob, a partner at FAT, explains that they modeled their idea after business parks. The huts allow for "the kinds of activities that usually happen buried deep within

a community," and have already been used by a group that makes model boats and as a space for music lessons. —ZR

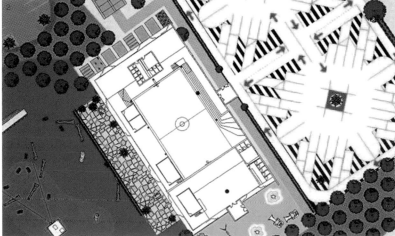

1 Cultural park, Hoogvliet, the Netherlands   2 Hoogvliet site plan   3 Hoogvliet model

Homerton Struggle Niche

Nils Norman   London, United Kingdom   2005

"I am interested in the mechanisms of gentrification and regeneration," says London-based artist Nils Norman, "and how play can act as an antidote to the increasingly paranoid climate of fear and control that is now part of how public spaces are conceptualized and designed." Norman, whose work straddles art, architecture, and urban planning, suggests that "pockets of disorder" are needed in today's commercially dominated urban planning schemes. His most recent art project, *The Homerton Playscape Multiple Struggle Niche*, was commissioned by City Projects, a London-based, non-profit arts organization and research center. The site-specific project was developed for Homerton in East London, an impoverished area that now borders the 2012 Olympics regeneration zone. City Projects commissioned Norman to create a project that would act as a foil to the huge wave of development already underway in the area.

Norman's point of departure was the existing Homerton Grove Adventure Playground, one of the few remaining adventure playgrounds in the world. He proposed extending the site to create a self-build park for the community that would provide a space where adults and children could come together to conduct community-based experiments in urban planning as a counterpoint to the large-scale commercial and residential developments being considered for the area. The parkland would form part of a larger network of similarly disused local sites to create what Norman calls "a local network of informal DIY parks." Norman explains that his ultimate goal is to create "an interesting and disruptive experiment in city planning and a welcome antidote to the business-as-usual 'place-making' of city privatization." —ZR

1 Poster of Homerton Struggle Niche, London

2 Detail of Homerton Struggle Niche poster

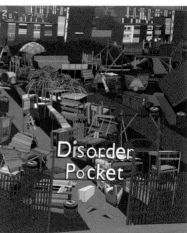

Alexanderplatz

RACA   Berlin, Germany   2005

As part of the 2005 *Urban Art Stories* exhibition, sponsored by arts organizations in Berlin, Copenhagen, and Malmö, graphic designer Pulsk Ravn and architect Johan Carlsson of RACA were invited to create a public art installation for Berlin's Alexanderplatz. Exhibition curator Petra Reichensperger writes, "No other public plaza is as strongly associated with Berlin." Known as "Alex," it was immortalized in Alfred Döblin's novel *Berlin Alexanderplatz* as the center of swinging 1920s nightlife, and is now a relic of 1960s socialist urban planning. The installation, which took place every day for a week, involved the artists dressing up in identical blue-and-white uniforms and setting up 100 blue deck chairs in the middle of the concrete square. The movable chairs provided a much-needed place for tourists and commuters to rest in the midst of the vast transit hub. As in their other work, this project involves "public service," a performance act that pokes fun at the social codes associated with particular situations. For *Alexanderplatz*, the artists would place the chairs at even distances apart in the middle of the square. Participants would then move them throughout the course of the day, in a small way reappropriating the space as their own. —Elise Youn

1 Installation in Alexanderplatz, Berlin

(PARK)ing   Rebar   San Francisco, California   2005

Ex-attorney and filmmaker Matthew Passmore started Rebar on a whim in 2004, when he invited friends John Bela (a landscape architect), Jed Olson (a doctor), and Judson Holt (a litigation consultant) to the New Mexico desert to build a public library for *Cabinet* magazine out of an actual filing cabinet. *PARK(ing)* consists of an instant "park" set up in two metered parking spaces in San Francisco's Financial District. In November 2005, Rebar "leased" the spaces from the city for a day by paying the parking meters, and then installed sod, a bench, and a potted tree for shade. *PARK(ing)* is a both a pleasant spot in which to relax and a political statement against the privatization of public space for automobile use. Although the park only lasted a couple of hours, Rebar documented the project extensively and posted the films and photographs on their website. *PARK(ing)* has since inspired similar performances in Santa Monica, California and Trapani, Italy.

For future PARK(ers), Rebar has created the "PARK(ing) Assembly Manual" with instructions on how to replicate the piece in any city. —EY

1 *PARK(ing)* installation, San Francisco, CA

2 Parking meters modified by Rebar

Guerilla Gardeners   Toronto Public Space Committee   Toronto, Canada   2003-
GuerrillaGardening.org   Richard Reynolds   London, United Kingdom   2004-

Inspired by the community activism of New York's Green Guerillas, today's guerrilla gardeners combine a rural gardening sensibility with an interest in beautifying neglected urban spaces. The Green Guerillas began in 1973, at a time when land values were depreciating, crime was rampant, and residents were leaving for the suburbs in droves. Lower East Side artist Liz Christy organized the takeover of an abandoned lot along the Bowery, converting it into a community vegetable garden. This first garden spawned an entire movement in which residents of low-income neighborhoods banded together to reclaim abandoned lots, transforming them into oases of green space.

GuerrillaGardening.org in London and Guerilla Gardeners in Toronto have similar goals, although their publicity is very 21st-century, relying on websites, mass emailing, and SMS text-messaging to get the word out about their events. The groups plant neglected traffic islands, spruce up public planters, and weed the soil

around sidewalk trees, mostly at night and on weekends in convenient areas, as many of their members have day jobs. To encourage local community participation, Toronto's Guerilla Gardeners post signs saying "please water me" next to their plantings, and London's GuerrillaGardening.org ask area merchants to pick up trash around the flowers. According to Richard Reynolds of the London group, the idea is as simple as finding a bald spot of dirt, digging a hole, and dropping in some seeds: "Local people can take this on themselves, together as communities." —EY

1 Guerilla Gardeners planting in Toronto, Canada

2 GuerrillaGardening.org event in London, United Kingdom

Coventry Phoenix Initiative   MacCormac Jamieson Prichard   Coventry, United Kingdom   2004

The Coventry Phoenix Initiative aptly takes its name from the mythical bird that dies in flames and later rises from the ashes. Coventry's historic medieval core suffered severe damage from German air raids during World War II, and in the years following the war, the city continued to decline as a result of insensitive town planning and a long recession. In 1997, the city council applied for funding to create a master plan to connect its three landmark cathedrals to Coventry's second-most popular attraction, the National Museum of Road Transport. London-based firm MacCormac Jamieson Prichard (MJP) won the competition by proposing a continuum of pedestrian-friendly spaces—providing the backdrop for eight public art installations while also setting the stage for future investment and development.

MJP's seven-acre master plan links 1,000 years of Coventry history and infuses the renewed spaces with public art. As part of the plan to "tell the story of Coventry" through public spaces, art, and architecture, MJP worked with archaeologists to excavate the cathedral and priory grounds, leaving some of the remains on display in a garden-like atmosphere. In the newly reconstructed Priory Cloister and Garden, *Here*, a sound installation by David Ward, plays recorded memories of Coventry residents from eight outdoor speakers. From Priory Place, a collection of new low-rise residential and commercial buildings around a small piazza, visitors can see the *Whittle Arches*, by artist Alex Beleschenko. Named in honor of the inventor of the jet engine who was born in Coventry, the two 50-foot-high glass-enclosed steel spans reach from the northern tip of the piazza to the far corners of Millennium Place, a new public square, and the site of a number of public art installations. Two of the most thoughtful pieces are by Berlin-born artist Jochen Gerz. *Public Bench* is a 147-foot-long curved bench commemorating meetings, friendships, or memorable encounters. For this project, the artist instructed participants to record their names and a date on a small red plaque, to be installed randomly on the white bench, as one resident noted, like

"freckles on the cheeks of the city." For *Future Monument*, Gerz asked various community groups to dedicate a plaque to a group of people who were once considered enemies, but are now friends. Installed beside a fractured-glass obelisk, the plaques read, "To our German friends," "To our Russian friends," and even, "To our British friends." The theme of reconciliation runs through many of the works in the Phoenix Initiative, reflecting both Coventry's history and hopes for regeneration. —EY

1, 2, 3 Millennium Place, Coventry Phoenix Initiative, Coventry, United Kingdom

Public Art Projects

Greyworld

UK, Ireland, France, Germany 1996-05

Composer Andrew Shoben founded Greyworld in 1993 together with three other artists and designers with the goal of "transforming the grey areas of the city, which we usually ignore, into a magical world." Greyworld's projects bring together design, digital technology, and sound to "articulate" everyday public spaces, injecting commonly ignored urban objects with a friendly, interactive "personality."

Railings, a temporary installation for Paris, London, and Berlin, is a set of otherwise conventional metal sidewalk railings that play the tune, "The Girl from Ipanema," when struck with an umbrella or stick. *Bridge 2* consists of a bright blue carpet installed along the length of a ped-estrian footbridge across the river Liffey in Dublin. When people cross over the bridge, sensors in the carpet trigger unexpected sounds, such as footsteps crunching in snow, splashing through water, or walking through fallen leaves.

Bins and Benches is set in a newly redeveloped plaza in Cambridge, England. Integrated with sensors, four park benches and five trash bins are mechanized to move around the square in response to changes in weather, the number of people in the plaza, and the time of day. The benches, for instance, cluster together when the plaza is crowded, while the bins line up at trash collection time. On sunny days, the benches "sing," and on rainy days, the bins "shiver" from the chill. Greyworld believes that personalizing urban objects creates a sense of intimacy between people and their surrounding environment. —EY

1 Musical railings, London, United Kingdom

Solkan Fountain

Sadar Vuga Arhitekti

Solkan, Slovenia 2001

The Solkan Fountain was inaugurated in 2001 on the one thousandth anni-versary of the alpine town of Solkan. Situated on the Slovene-Italian border, along the river Soča, Solkan, like many towns in the region, has a long and contested history. Through it all, however, the Soča and the surrounding landscape have remained lasting symbols of Solkan. Ljubljana-based Sadar Vuga Arhitekti were inspired by this resiliency when designing the fountain, which resembles both a sculpted infinity symbol as well as a ripple of the river itself. Formed from a concrete shell clad with specially cut blue-green granite, the fountain, like the landscape, has come to be seen as a defining symbol of the town center. —EY

1 Solkan Fountain, Solkan, Slovenia

Park Bench House

Sean Godsell Architects

Melbourne, Australia 2002

Melbourne has twice ranked first in "The World's Most Livable Cities" index, an annual survey by *The Economist*. In recent years though, this sprawling city of 6.7 million has grown to include approximately 4,000 homeless people. Each night hundreds of homeless sleep outdoors, appropriating the city's public parks as informal accommodation. While the majority of Melbourne's park furniture aims to deter people from sleeping on it, the Park Bench House actually encourages people to spend the night there. During the day, the bench's steel structure supports an aluminum platform upon which visitors can sit. At night, the platform lifts up to form a slanted roof, revealing a stainless-steel mesh "bed" underneath. A photovoltaic cell nightlight, attached to the rear of the bench, shines when the bed is occupied. —EY

1 Park Bench House, Melbourne, Australia

Römerkastell & Marktplatz   Dietrich Brennenstuhl & Nimbus Design   Stuttgart, Germany   2003

The soft-hued, oversized living room lamps by Dietrich Brennenstuhl and Nimbus Design add a warm, relaxed atmosphere to Stuttgart's Römerkastell and Marktplatz areas. Brennenstuhl began by installing a loose 40-by-40-foot grid of the shaded lamps in front of the Römerkastell Event Hall, a recently renovated concert venue. The new street lamps invite people to change the color of their lighting by tugging at an old-fashioned pull-chain. The event hall grounds, once deserted and unwelcoming, particularly at night, now feel inviting and playful. Brennenstuhl also directed the temporary installation

of several of the lamps in Stuttgart's historic central marketplace, as part of a city government initiative to redesign the square, transforming it into a

popular gathering place for people at all hours. —EY

1 Römerkastell light installation, Stuttgart, Germany

Public Art Projects   Cliostraat   Siena and Udine, Italy   2001, 2005

Cliostraat was founded in 1991 in Turin, Italy to explore the in-between spaces of cities, "the realm of contemporary urban territories," where people interact directly with the urban environment and with each other. For *Play or Rewind*, Cliostraat redrew the lines of three playing fields—for soccer, volleyball, and bowling—laying them over three public squares in the historic town of Siena, Italy. The lines do not correspond with the plans of the squares, but rather extend diagonally across them and up building façades. Furnished with extra-large play equipment, the distorted playing

fields inspire both tourists and residents to take part in casual pick-up games, reinventing the rules to fit the new space.

Slacklines, a temporary installation for the 2005 "Luna Park. Arte Fantastica" exhibition at the Villa Manin Centro d'Arte Contemporanea in Udine, employs the flexible nylon cords used in slacklining, a sport similar to tightrope-walking, to generate a web of hammocks on which museum visitors can sit and relax. The ropes, suspended from trees in a nearby grove, are woven together to evoke a horizontal spider's web, an impression

confirmed by the giant, hairy spider hanging from above. —EY

1 *Play or Rewind* volleyball game, Siena, Italy

Jumping Field   Tommi Grönlund/Petteri Nisunen   Helsinki, Finland   2000

For the "Under the Same Sky" public art exhibition at the Kiasma Museum of Contemporary Art, Tommi Grönlund and Petteri Nisunen constructed a 40-by-40-foot plywood platform, covered it with artificial grass, and supported it with van springs. Embedded in an existing field at the southeast tip of a manmade industrial peninsula in Helsinki, *Jumping Field* appears from afar to be part of the grass landscape. Upon closer examination however, the color and density of the turf reveal that *Jumping Field* is indeed a constructed fake. Grönlund and Nisunen created *Jumping Field* to resemble an actual playing field, but

with its odd dimensions and springy instability, it does not accommodate any traditional game. Nevertheless, people invented new ways to use it and

it was extremely popular during the three months of the exhibition. —EY

1 *Jumping Field*, Helsinki, Finland

the 24-hour city

In 1961, the American urban theorist Jane Jacobs aptly noted four conditions for creating a thriving city that is inclusive of people of all ages, backgrounds, and interests. The first is a mix of buildings and spaces for living and working. The second is a diversity of people and uses. The third is human-scale urban planning and design, and the fourth is a mix of old and new buildings combined. Architects and designers continue to reference Jacobs' methods when thinking about generating diversity, enhancing the safety of cities, and encouraging a melting pot of people, ideas, exchanges, and interactions. Through an integrated approach, *The 24-Hour City* meshes residential and commercial, public and private, cultural and recreational, programmed and unprogrammed, to encourage expectation and anticipation, and to incite us to share in the experiences that enhance our everyday lives, 24/7.

The projects presented here are examples of how underutilized public spaces are being reinvented with bold new designs that will activate the contemporary urban landscape through the day and night. In Taichung, Taiwan, a new popular music venue is being designed with an outdoor amphitheater that can be used for concerts at night and recreational activities during the day, ensuring the site is energized before and after performances. In New York City, similar efforts geared towards enhancing activity and accessibility before and after the curtain call are guiding the redesign of an iconic performance district with new picnic lawns, restaurants, and legible open spaces. Two projects in London, one on a post-industrial wasteland and another in a low-income neighborhood, are providing new town squares to encourage local activities that will generate new identities for these burgeoning mixed-use districts. In Dublin, New York, and the Croatian city of Split, formerly industrial waterfronts are being reconceived as new mixed-use neighborhoods and downtown districts marked by cultural, recreational, and commercial spaces that will enliven the area and encourage the creation of new perpetually active urban destinations. These bold designs take advantage of existing infrastructure and harness local interests and resources in order to engage a diversity of people and activities, encourage both formal and informal happenings, and foster social exchange, all essential components of a thriving 24-hour urban place. —ZR

roundtable discussion

donald bates
principal, LAB architecture studio

gregg pasquarelli
partner, SHoP architects

charles renfro
partner, diller scofidio + renfro

craig schwitter
partner, buro happold engineers and VAI trustee

marilyn taylor
chair, skidmore owings & merrill

marc tsurumaki
principal, lewis.tsurumaki.lewis architects
and VAI trustee

*The following conversation took place in
spring 2005 at Van Alen Institute. This text is
an edited version of the original transcript.*

tsurumaki When I talk about the 24-hour
City, I mean a place that has a mix of uses for
different people at different times. What do
other people think?

bates In my experience, creating a successful
24-hour city has a lot to do with the commercial
development. There are imperatives in terms of
profit and property ownership. In most American
cities, the end of the development is literally at
the property line. In comparison, our experience
of designing Federation Square in Australia was
that the local government organizations made
a serious effort and investment to blur that edge
beyond the property line. In Melbourne, city
planners have upgraded the neighborhoods around
entirely commercial projects in order to allow for
interchange between neighborhoods and people.

renfro Barcelona takes its urban design very
seriously. Huge strides have been made to initiate
different types of developments that encourage
connectivity, exchange, and a mix of uses, 24
hours a day, across the city.
It is interesting to explore what makes
Barcelona successful. They began with a
tight medieval city and really made a specific
commitment to public space, which clearly deals
with Catalan culture. They are people that love
being out on the streets. But it also has to do with
the fact that they have a city architect, currently
Josep Acebillo Marin. The notion that there is
a city architect, somebody who is responsible for
the large scale and intermediate form of the city,
really makes a difference.
The other thing that is interesting about
Barcelona is the attitude that the city architect is
important and can make changes that extend not
just to tourist sites or the wealthy neighborhoods
but stretch through all the economic levels of the
city. It is a wonderful achievement.

bates In the United Kingdom, "mixed-use" also
means having a mix of incomes. This is a man-
dated part of every new development. In order to
get a building permit you have to have a mix
of socioeconomic levels. However, what can also

define a successful mixed-use neighborhood in addition to parks, cultural institutions, and educational buildings is commercial space. For example, when you go to Fort Worth, there is the beautiful Kimball Art Museum designed by Louis I. Kahn, and the Modern Art Museum of Fort Worth designed by Tadao Ando, but there is nothing else around there. If you do not want to eat in the restaurants of those museums, there is no place to eat and there is nothing to attract people who are not visiting these buildings.

renfro On the one hand, recreational spaces in the city emerge without any external forces or legislation. On the other hand, they are a product of commercial interests. Yet they can both allow for new social formations to occur. Recreation encompasses a broad range of behaviors and activities from the more predetermined types, found in legislated spaces, to the more spontaneous types found in loose environments. There are parallels with the definitions of games and play, between the idea of control through a rigid set of rules that define a game as opposed to the improvisation, invention, and freedom of play. Both of these things should be allowed to occur in cities; that is what makes urban places so fascinating.

pasquarelli While working on the master plan for the East River Waterfront here in New York, we found it interesting that whenever we proposed "mixed-use" to the community, they were immediately afraid it would change or destroy the quality of their neighborhoods. We believe that an intense mixture of uses was necessary to make the neighborhoods thrive and reverse many of the problems these communities are facing. I think one problem communities have is with the term "mixed-use" itself. Its meaning and its effects really need to be further defined. In Europe, there is a greater understanding of what this term can mean culturally, and in Asia, it is simply a productive fact of urban life. The culture accepts that "mixed-use" and vibrancy is a good thing for city planning. Here, we have been slower to understand this and that is why you end up with texture-less places.

Terrorism hasn't helped. The fear of being in high-risk locations—primarily dense cities—has created a level of fear which is being countered with concepts for making cities less dense. I think this is wrong and simply a defense mechanism rather than a solution.

taylor The East River Waterfront, which we planned for the Downtown Alliance and Community Board 1 for the area south of Gregg's plan, from the Brooklyn Bridge to Battery Park City, is a great example of how thoroughly land uses can be mixed as we reclaim waterfront areas. Residents, visitors, businesses, and office workers can live together and need not be separated in the way 20th-century zoning dictated. New zoning techniques encourage the interaction and connectivity essential to urban vitality and sustainability. This breathes life back into the public realm because everyone uses it everyday.

bates Transportation plays a role in creating destinations in the city and encouraging thriving public spaces. In Nottingham in England, for example, they have recently introduced a tram system that is really changing the nature of the city. First of all it is inclusive to everyone. It is also forging connections through the city that are changing the way the city operates. You can move around the city much faster and get to different neighborhoods, which might have been out of reach before. "Mixed-use" implies densification to me and the ability to have efficient public transportation, which is positive for the environment, and also for the city, encouraging new development across the urban frame. We need more projects like this that help animate the city by fostering connections and accessibility.

taylor Well-planned public transportation is a great contributor to the shared space and public life that are essential elements of the successful "mixed-use" city. But for many decades in the United States and in new "quick-growth" cities, the emphasis has been on roads for cars which remove us from participating in the life of the public realm.

Other cities offer better results. In Hong Kong, for example, extensions to subway and railroad lines are integrally tied with public investments such as the new airport at Chek Lop Kok and with private investments, including the new towns and town centers. Land sales for directed private development add to the resources for creating a robust network of public transportation. Such coordinated planning supports the vitality and sustainability of the "mixed-use" city.

pasquarelli It is again a question of density as an essential component of a city. If you say to people, "Are you for sustainability?" They say, "Yes." If you say, "Are you for protecting the environment?" They say, "Yes." If you say, "Are you for density?" They say, "Absolutely not." I think the term needs to be redefined and even then it will take time for people to understand the benefits so we can move forward in a positive direction that is more sustainable.

tsurumaki Which projects in the United States are taking risks? The High Line in New York City is a great example. To make a park on the elevated railroad that runs across 25 city blocks instead of tearing down the structure is a visionary concept for the city. The High Line is also very bold because it is intentionally a slow space and is not intended to be overly programmed with activities and events.

taylor That's what makes the project so radical. A discussion that is important to public space, and one that too often gets overlooked, is its capacity to better accommodate temporal use. To what extent do different uses at different times of day play into city life? How does one design territories that can change to accommodate different activities, at various times, for different forms of occupancy?

schwitter One thing that we are finding is starting to help encourage diversity is the development of sustainability guidelines in cities such as London. The city's guidelines include a section about environmental issues and low energy but the other two-thirds of the book are actually about socioeconomic issues: economic activity,

production of jobs, low-income housing. These types of things are all seen in the framework of talking about sustainability in England right now. Therefore, "mixed-use" or a 24-hour city is seen as a sustainable model for an urban place.

bates I think that the separation of uses and single-use zoning was generated out of a reaction to the industrial city and came out of early modernist imperatives towards a hyper-organization of space. I think the architects and people of our generation assume that a diverse program is a positive thing and almost a pre-requisite of urban design. I think that urbanity or vital city planning cannot be reduced to a simple formulaic set of conditions. Density and diversity alone and the idea of mixed-use in and of itself aren't necessarily sufficient.

renfro What do "mixed-use," "24-hour," "multi-functional" mean? Take Lincoln Center for the Performing Arts; it was conceived as a mega-block. It was one of the first projects of its type when it was created in 1960 and paved the way for similar projects such as the Barbican in London. It was a tailored landscape that separated the pedestrians and cars, and made new experiences for each of them that were previously unavailable within the context of the city. The project failed on the car front—they could have made the tunnel on 65th Street quite interesting for vehicular traffic. However, they did succeed to a certain degree, from a pedestrian standpoint. There is a broad, rarified, silent, amazingly contemplative landscape at Lincoln Center, particularly on the North Plaza. While serene spaces don't typically define the 24-hour city, they are important and powerful precisely in their opposition to the frenetic quality of the city. In Lincoln Center's current state of disrepair, it is easy to overlook the power of its austerity. Our initial mandate when thinking about the redevelopment of Lincoln Center was to make 65th Street a street again—to reveal the mix of activities that are already present in the complex and to capitalize on the energy and excitement within the performance venues. I hope that our design succeeds in doing both things at once: maintaining a dignified and distinct public space, but also opening up Lincoln Center to the city. We have resisted the tendency towards commercialization. Instead I hope that we have been able to build an experience that is unique to this location.

pasquarelli The performative quality of architecture is what matters the most. When people ask for retail, it is not always because they really want another place to shop, but it is a word that they equate with activity or texture versus something that is harder to define, such as delight in a space, or things that interest you or activate the mind. I think this is what makes 24-hour space so difficult to define. Is it just different programs? Or is it differentiated performative spaces? Can it be both public and private? Can it be a blend of things in between, and how does one begin to make places and architecture that allow for all of that difference to occur without it being so defined? For the East River Waterfront project we are focusing on making both private and public spaces so that different types of environments emerge. So the waterfront does not seem like a packaged mix of uses with a viewing platform there, a store there, a square there, and a building there. We wanted to take a more integrated approach that is sustainable and realizable. It is a much more subtle approach but creates a more nuanced environment and a richer range of experiences. For a huge part of the last year-and-a-half we did not design anything but spent time exploring how the performative qualities of the different spaces we envisioned might work together. I think it is this type of approach that make a city vibrant.

tsurumaki One of the issues to consider is to what degree the spaces are pre-legislated by their design or the architecture and the landscape. How are these spaces and buildings dictating the types of uses and activities that can occur? To what degree can they be inhabited in other ways or misappropriated? Can they be taken over opportunistically by the public and is it possible to design spaces in such a way that they allow for

that kind of performative interaction rather than a kind of legislation of activities?

renfro One of my goals as an architect is to produce projects that defy expectation. Spaces are organized to sponsor spontaneous activities and unexpected discoveries as much as they are to accommodate the intended program. All the elements work together in an integrated fashion to provide a complete experience.

schwitter We should be creating cities that ensure that new public spaces are inclusive and encourage inhabitation by different types of people.

tsurumaki But can you design or legislate that a public place must be inclusive to all? I don't think you can.

renfro What one person defines as potentially exclusive might not be perceived as such by someone else.

bates To me, "24-hour" or "mixed-use" are not only ecologically sustainable terms but are also economical. It is logical to have many different sorts of activities in a city so that when there Is an economic downturn they do not all disappear, making a place no longer viable. A city needs a heterogeneous enough mix that something else will take over. Unless you have that, you run the risk of creating a city with no means to renew its strength or character, or adapt to change.

Contemporary Music Center Stan Allen Architects   Taichung, Taiwan   2008

In 2004, the Taiwanese city of Taichung selected Stan Allen Architects (SAA) to design a new Contemporary Music Center (CMC) as a response to the growing interest in Asian popular music. Taichung, located in the center of the country, is the second-largest city with a population of one million. Taichung has no designated cultural district and arts and music venues are scattered throughout the city. The CMC site is in an area southwest of the city undergoing extensive redevelopment. It was chosen for its accessibility, as it is easily reached by train or via a major highway. A residential complex is planned for a site south of the CMC; while a sports field, arts and technology center, extreme sports forest, open market, and playgrounds will be built to the north.

The brief for the project was to create an event space centered around an outdoor auditorium for 18,000 spectators. SAA devised an architectural strategy that would enliven the nondescript site and provide an integrated series of spaces to accommodate a manifold program that would generate activity 24 hours a day. Allen asserts that he focused on "designing and articulating the functional and architectural relationships between programs to make sure that the site was active around the clock." Taking the idea of an events landscape, SAA conceived an artificial topography in which the auditorium and three recital halls, as well as workspaces such as sound labs and studios, some with informal performance spaces, are arranged around what SAA refers to as a "horizontal skyscraper that complements and completes the landform, giving a strong architectural identity to the site." This bridge-like structure houses the educational facilities and is wrapped with screens and projections that animate the architecture. A concourse embedded within the artificial landscape services the complex but is invisible from ground level, maintaining a clear focus on the performance venues above. Allen explains that his "ambition was to create an architecture that was informed by landscape but does not mimic landscape...a new

form of public space, a charged and activated space." Key to his design was a reinterpretation of traditional squares or piazzas and their formal codes of behavior. Instead, the CMC is a new type of public space, which encourages improvisation and reinvention though a flexible, open-plan design with programs arranged randomly to accommodate change over time. —ZR

1 Contemporary Music
Center, Taichung, Taiwan
2 Program distribution
diagram
3 Crowd at CMC
music venue
4 Entrance to CMC
5 Section of CMC

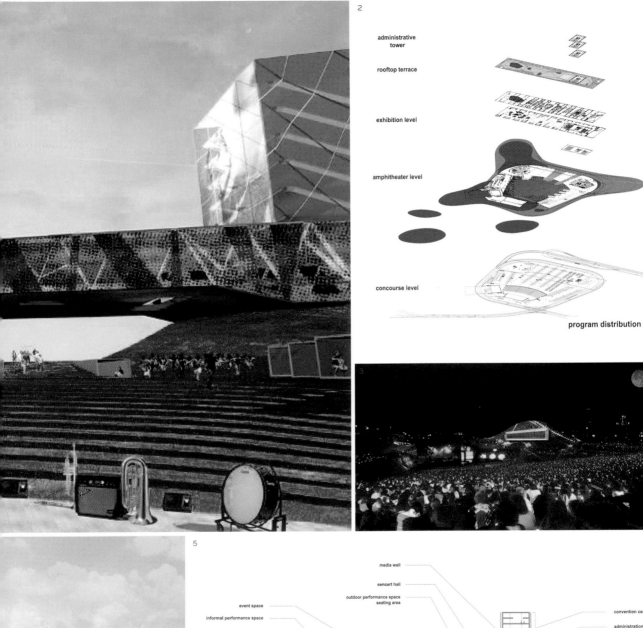

2

administrative tower

rooftop terrace

exhibition level

amphitheater level

concourse level

program distribution

3

5

media wall

concert hall

outdoor performance space
seating area

event space

informal performance space

cafe

R+D floor

exhibition floor

convention center

administration offices

recital hall 1
rehearsal space

city balcony

foyer 1

foyer 2

support/service
loading/unloading
parking

car parking

car parking

Flux Park, King's Cross

General Public Agency   London, United Kingdom   2012

General Public Agency (GPA), based in London, is a unique multi-disciplinary consultancy working on urban and rural renewal projects. The firm, which encompasses architects, planners, curators, and artists, is headed by Lucy Musgrave, former director of the Architecture Foundation in London, and Clare Cumberlidge, a curator and writer.

Their work is primarily focused on strategic visioning for places undergoing intense regeneration with emphasis placed on the importance of culture and the arts. Since 2003, they have been working with London developers Argent on the King's Cross

Central redevelopment, a 65-acre brownfield site situated between and to the north of King's Cross and St. Pancras stations. The $3.5 billion scheme for the entire area includes a mix of houses, offices, cultural institutions, and recreational facilities that will animate the neighborhood throughout the day and night, and create a new district for the city. Over 40% of the area has been designated as public space with three new parks, five squares, and 20 streets.

King's Cross is known primarily as a void within the heart of London—an industrial center surrounded by abandoned railway lines. This project

aims to reclaim these spaces and transform them for public use. GPA's strategy takes advantage of the existing terrain of abandoned spaces with their own ecologies and histories and infuses them with new uses and identities to create a multi-layered landscape, an "urban pleasure garden." The overarching theme of the project is play, which GPA defines as, "a non-age-specific synonym for spontaneous behavior, something which exists everywhere but in the public realm is rarely encouraged and often actively discouraged." For GPA, "play should permeate the entire site."

After extensive analysis, community workshops, and mappings of the site which pinpointed key stakeholders, GPA commissioned a variety of practitioners including artists, multi-media designers, and even a horticulturalist. GPA's proposal also includes a central programmed space for cultural, recreational, and leisure activities: Flux Park, designed in association with British architects Allies & Morrison and engineers Arup, is intended to enliven the area through the day and night and be a focal point for the community, a new public square with views across the city.

Included in the park proposal is the transformation of a former gasholder into a ramped space with 7,300 square feet of usable space for public and private events. GPA's vision is to "achieve a new structure within the old which equals the original in terms of civic presence, design elegance and structural ingenuity."

Inspired by ramped spaces such as Frank Lloyd Wright's Guggenheim Museum in New York, GPA's design turns the gasholder into a multi-functional space accessible on foot or by elevator. Together, the different levels will house an auditorium with play zones, function rooms available for

community activities, a public platform for gatherings or performances. The top floor is to be a viewing platform. The gasholder is envisioned as a semi-open structure, and playing fields at the base will integrate it into the larger King's Cross scheme.

GPA's design takes advantage of an ordinary gasholder, and adaptively reuses this familiar structure to create a new type of public space that will generate activities at all times of the day, week, and season. —ZR

1 Flux Park, King's Cross, London, United Kingdom 2, 3 Concept sketches for Flux Park 4 Aerial view of King's Cross, looking north, showing Flux Park at center 5 Site plan of Flux Park

2
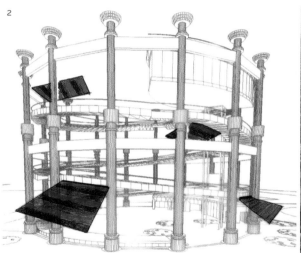

3
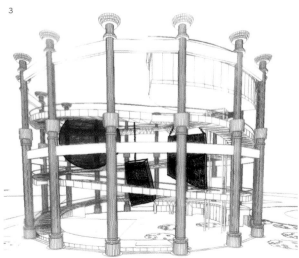

4

5
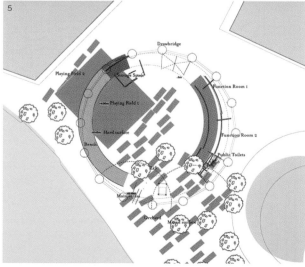

North Plaza, Lincoln Center   Diller Scofidio + Renfro   New York, New York   2009

In April 2004, Lincoln Center unveiled its design for a "Street of the Arts." The new vision, the brainchild of New York-based architects Diller Scofidio + Renfro, lighting designers L'Observatoire International, and graphic designers 2×4, with FXFowle Architects, attempts to open up this mega-block cultural facility and activate the public spaces threaded throughout the performance halls to create a thriving 24-hour district. Elizabeth Diller explains that, "The challenge is to interpret the genetic code of this 'Monumental Modernism' into a language for younger, more diverse audiences following generations of cultural and political change." Built in the 1960s by a team led by Wallace K. Harrison, Lincoln Center's modern architecture is all grand-scale public plazas and monumental buildings that do not encourage foot traffic and have few intimate spaces for lingering and gathering. The major avenues and streets all around also do not encourage foot traffic. Diller's goal is to extend "the intensity within the performance halls into the mute public spaces between those halls and the surrounding streets."

Key aspects of the design include expanding and opening up entrance lobbies to Alice Tully Hall in the Juilliard School and adding a new dance studio at the top of the space with a transparent façade allowing visitors to watch dancers practicing and warming up for performances. The Film Society's new complex will have an increased street presence and a new glass façade will be added to the Vivian Beaumont and Mitzi E. Newhouse Theaters. West 65th Street, between Broadway and Amsterdam Avenue, will be one car lane narrower and the sidewalk will be widened to encourage foot traffic.

The grand stairway leading to the plaza from 65th Street will be widened and will slope more gradually to allow for unobstructed views. LED displays embedded into the stairs will provide information about programs and performances. Central to the designers' concept is the enhancement of the North Plaza, the main public gathering space at the heart of Lincoln Center. DS+R have also introduced a new campus green, a 10,500-square-foot elevated lawn oriented towards the

reflecting pool that provides a space for gathering and relaxing during the day and at night. It also provides a "soft-scape" among the hard surfaces of Lincoln Center. A restaurant will be housed underneath the lawn with outdoor seating. Planting trees on the site, which will be lit at night, will further soften the space. Groups of seats arranged at the base of the trees will encourage lingering and offer shaded areas for relaxing in the summer. Charles Renfro asserts that "the design will strip off the foreboding and elitist walls of Lincoln Center, welcoming for the first time a large, disparate, and non-ticketed population

of New Yorkers and revealing the round-the-clock activities found deep within the existing structures."

Rather than designing an entirely new complex of buildings and spaces for Lincoln Center, the design team took advantage of the existing iconic design of the site. Through subtle shifts in scale and by improving accessibility to buildings and public spaces, as well as opening them up visually, the new design aims to activate the site 24/7.
—ZR

1 View of North Plaza from theater, New York, New York 2 The elevated lawn in North Plaza 3 The restaurant in North Plaza 4 North Plaza

Barking Town Square

muf architecture/art   London, United Kingdom   2007

In 2001, the London Borough of Barking and Dagenham Council developed an urban renewal strategy titled "An Urban Renaissance in East London." The initiative, which engaged both the public and private sectors, called for developments that would introduce new housing, cafés, shops, bars, restaurants, street improvements, and transportation links to the area. In 2005, Barking Town Square was selected as the focus of a series of studies and new developments. Along with a master plan, a new library and learning center, residences, and a new streetscape, muf, an art and architecture collective based in London, was commissioned to design the public realm.

Barking is an area with a low-income population and home to increasing numbers of immigrants from Eastern Europe. Muf was charged with creating a new town square that would help unite the community and integrate existing buildings—including the town hall—in with the new developments. Muf explains that the challenge was how to encourage

"aspirations to create a public realm peopled by young professionals chatting animatedly over their frappuccinos" while at the same time curbing "anxiety about young people loitering in public space and the ever-widening definition of what constitutes anti-social behavior."

Their solution is defined by a 68,000-square-foot central gathering and event space open all day and night. Muf's design consists of two contrasting yet interlocked spaces. The first is a hard landscape in front of the town hall and library and the second is an urban arboretum, an "artificial forest" of carefully selected trees between the library and new buildings. Where the two spaces meet is a large gathering place with seating. Muf's Liza Fior comments that the "long side of the T will generally be in shadow due to the orientation of the new buildings so we proposed to exacerbate this condition. We were interested in the idea that mystery should have a place on the site alongside legibility." The resulting forest is a particularly interesting part of this project.

The arrangement of the trees has been carefully thought out to provide shade but to also allow ample daylight to pass through to illuminate the area. At night, a series of candelabra, hung from columns throughout the forest, will light the main square. In order to ensure that the spaces are utilized, muf is working with the organizations housed in the surrounding buildings to determine programs to engage people of all ages and backgrounds. They lobbied for a café to be relocated from within a building to a prominent corner of the site and linked to an arcade that provides a covered walkway to the town hall and to houses above. Muf's design is mindful of the needs of the community yet attempts to create a space that is unique, incorporating fresh ideas, like the urban forest. The variety of spaces will hopefully encourage interaction and exchange and help bind the community through shared activities day and night. —ZR

1 New Town Square,   2 Site plan
London, United Kingdom   3 Artifical forest

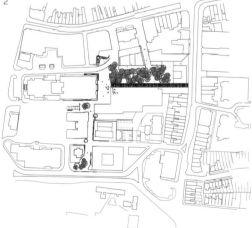

Grand Canal Square — Martha Schwartz (w/ Tiros Resources) — Dublin, Ireland — 2008

Grand Canal Square is the centerpiece of a new development on Dublin's former industrial docklands aimed at stimulating development in the southeast of the city. Known for Temple Bar, a thriving cultural quarter with a lively nightlife, Dublin has set a precedent as a city determined to create thriving districts that are activated throughout the day and night through a mix of uses and public spaces. The project includes a linear park that runs for half a mile along the banks of the Royal Canal with cycle and pedestrian lanes, seating, and public spaces that culminate in the Dublin Docklands Development located on Grand Canal.

The existing square that forms the heart of the project was built within the last ten years but has failed to create a focal point of activity. Martha Schwartz, based in Cambridge, Massachusetts, and Tiros Resources, a Dublin landscape architecture firm, have designed a bold new 10,000-square-foot plaza that aims to activate the space. The public square is located at the west end of the site, facing the water and is bordered by Grand Canal Theatre and Le Meridien hotel, both designed by Studio Daniel Libeskind.

Martha Schwartz is known for rethinking post-industrial sites. Recent projects have included landscapes for the Mesa Arts and Entertainment Center in Arizona, the Swiss Re Building in Munich, and Exchange Square in Manchester. For Grand Canal Square, a $10 million project, the major premise was to stretch the square beyond its boundary and into the adjacent buildings in an effort to generate activity inside and out. Borrowing from theater design, the metaphor of the red carpet is the defining element of the scheme. A red resin-glass pathway runs from the theater to the water, dividing the space diagonally. The opposite diagonal axis is characterized as a green carpet paved with green resin-glass. Red and green LEDs frame

the pathways at night to dramatic effect, enhanced by eight-foot light poles designed with Edinburgh-based Spiers and Major Associates that are programmed to randomly switch on and off creating a subtle play of color and light throughout the space. The square is built over an existing car park. In order to integrate plantings on the site, the designers had to incorporate low planting beds that are slotted into the red and green pathways. Some are ornamental and are planted with flowers and marshlike grass referencing the history of the site. Others are planted with grass-covered lawns for sitting and gathering. Crisscrossing the entire site is a bold pattern of granite paths that encourage movement in multiple directions and forge visual as well as physical connections between spaces and buildings. These pathways also delineate areas for performances and events. (A sloped space under the overhang of the theater has also been acoustically tuned for outdoor performances.)

In addition to a water feature made from white and green marble, triangular structures emerge from the ground at two points, rising to a height of 14 feet. Made from a transparent stainless steel mesh, their sculptural forms create points of visual interest but have functional properties allowing air into the car park below. Fitted with blue fluorescent lights, they glow at night and are visible from the buildings around the site. Shauna Gillies-Smith, the design principal for the project, explains that they "wanted to create a strong design that would have an active presence on the site." Through the playful use of color, texture, and light, the square is animated 24 hours a day making it a site for individual as well as group activity. —ZR

1 Grand Canal Square at dusk, Dublin, Ireland
2 Detail of Grand
Canal Square showing pathways and light posts
3 Site plan

East River Waterfront Study SHoP and Richard Rogers Partnership New York, New York 2009

Although Manhattan is surrounded on three sides by water, there exist few opportunities for gaining access to the East River, which retains the warehouses and piers of its industrial past. It is blocked by the F.D.R. Drive, an elevated highway that was built in the 1930s and divides the city from the water. In 2004, as part of Mayor Bloomberg's larger vision to create a network of greenways around the city and as part of revitalization initiatives for Lower Manhattan, New York's SHoP Architects and London's Richard Rogers Partnership were selected from an open competition to design a master plan for the area to revitalize this underutilized stretch of space and create a thriving 24-hour mixed-use waterfront district. In 2005, after more than 70 presentations to community groups, city officials, and government entities, the team officially announced their design. They had eliminated some of the more radical aspects of the plan, such as the residential towers that they had proposed to build over the F.D.R. Drive to help fund their scheme. The overall goal, however, remained the same: to reconnect the city with the waterfront and create linkages between the five neigh-borhoods that run the length of the river—Battery Park, the Financial District, South Street Seaport, the Civic Center, Chinatown, and the Lower East Side.

The team's design incorporates a series of interventions to energize the area with a variety of uses. A new two-mile esplanade and bicycle path, which will be 40 feet wide in places, is envisioned as the connective tissue linking Battery Park at the southern tip of Manhattan with East River Park further north. The esplanade will be lined with benches, planters, and tables.

Initial plans to remove the elevated highway proved too costly. Instead SHoP proposed cladding the façade to improve its appearance and acoustics, and the architects have developed a lighting system that will illuminate the underside. They have also made use of the structure of the highway as an architectural support for a series of glass pavilions for recreational and leisure facilities, retail outposts, and cultural venues.

Additional public spaces will be created along the waterfront by rebuilding Pier 15 to create a three-quarter-acre landscaped terrace over the water for larger gatherings and activities. Former boat slips along the water are also being reclaimed for new uses with pools for paddling in summer and skating rinks in winter.

The project, estimated to cost $150 million, is awaiting final approval. Set to break ground next year and be completed by 2012, it will be a major contribution to the revitalization of Lower Manhattan. —ZR

1 Aerial view, East River Waterfront Study, NY 2 Concept for Pier 42 beach 3 Concept for canoe launch 4 Joggers under elevated highway 5 Waterfront activities 6 Pool concept

Riva-Split Waterfront

3LHD Architects

Split, Croatia

2007

In March 2005, Zagreb architecture office 3LHD won an open competition to design a new $8 million waterfront development along the promenade in Split, Croatia's second largest city. The area is a UNESCO World Heritage Site and is bordered to the north by the Emperor Diocletian's Palace, built in 295 AD. Informally planned, the promenade area is nonetheless packed with markets, festivals, gatherings, sports events, and other social activities competing for space day and night. Initiated by the City of Split, the competition called for a new vision for the site that would tie together formal and informal activities and create a network of spaces that would further facilitate and encourage a confluence of activities 24 hours a day.

3LHD approached the project with an attitude that less is more. "We did not want to add another layer to the existing historical layers but instead create a neutral stage that would release the potential of the site without interfering too much." Their main concept is a new surface treatment that will unify the 300,000-square-foot area along the promenade. Inspired by patterns in Diocletian's Palace, 3LHD created a modulated pavement of colored tiles that reflects the light and changes color depending on the weather and time of day. Principal Saša Begović explains that this surface creates the "background for all of the existing and future facilities...defining the territory was key." Accordingly, light sources are built into the surface of the promenade so they do not obstruct the view. They break up the space, marking focal points where activity can occur.

Within this new landscape, 3LHD have introduced a marketplace, a performance area for concerts, and play spaces such as an interactive fountain. The restaurants, cafés, and amenities alongside the edge of the site are being upgraded with terraces for seating and gathering. 3LHD has also designed some new urban elements including a series of canopies to provide shelter from the wind and rain, which can be removed to open up the spaces for festivals and larger events.

The promenade culminates in a stepped edge of varying heights

that leads down to the water. Every space is angled toward the water and obstructions are kept to a minimum. Begović notes that, "the goal of the project is to try and emphasize and tune up all those events that are happening

right now on this urban, public, open, and accessible place." —ZR

1, 2 Riva-Split Waterfront, Split, Croatia 3 New paving and landscaping for Riva-Split Waterfront 4 Aerial view of Riva-Split Waterfront 5 Fountains at Riva-Split Waterfront

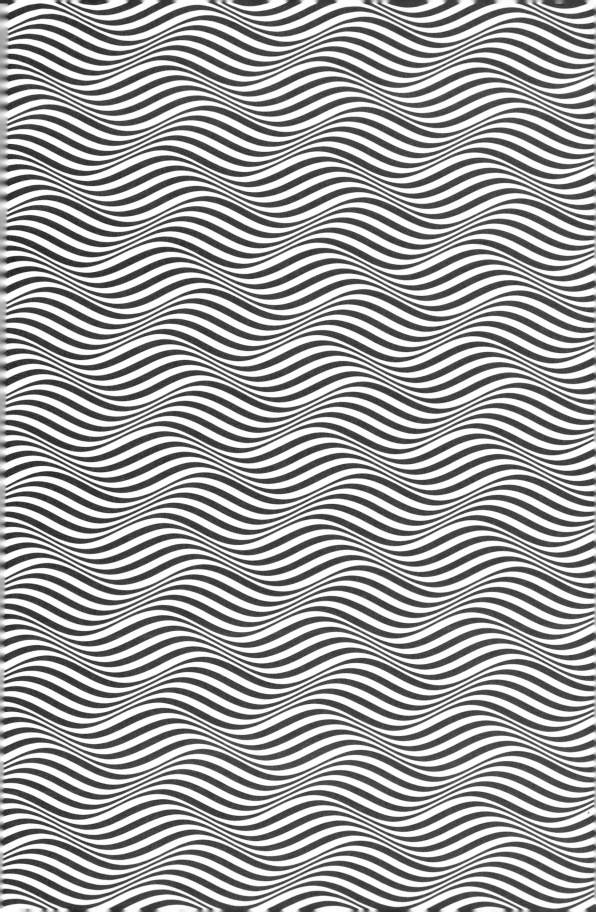

the
fun
city

Play is an essential part of human nature and is proven to profoundly benefit the psychological, physical, and emotional development of both children and adults. Dutch art historian Liane Lefaivre writes, play spaces can greatly increase "the livability of a city as they are pre-eminently meeting places for people of different ages and backgrounds." In spite of this, our increasingly structured lives continue to challenge opportunities for free play and heightened security concerns, safety issues, and fear of legal responsibility have brought about a decline in access to playgrounds that allow for exploration which stimulates the mind and encourages creativity. The projects presented here illustrate how architects, designers, landscape architects, and artists have taken up the cause, believing firmly in the fundamental importance of integrating new public spaces for recreation and play into our cities as an antidote to our increasingly complex urban environments. Fostering play, relaxation, education, and community interaction, these spaces re-envision the urban experience and provide opportunities for cultural and social exchange.

Whether formal or unofficial, interstitial or on the edge, *The Fun City* projects energize the public realm for people of all ages and backgrounds. In San Juan, Copenhagen, and the Japanese cities of Tachikawa and Obihiro, new fun landscapes include an extreme sports park that can be enjoyed by participants and spectators, a playscape in the sky with 24/7 activities and events, and an innovative new park with artificial surfaces for play, education, and exploration. Smaller-scale projects show possibilities for new playgrounds that go beyond typical designs, integrating sound, light, inventive materials, and custom-made play equipment, encouraging individual and group activities. Since Paris sought to make life more bearable during the hot summer months by creating an urban beach in its center, other cities worldwide have been inspired to create summertime getaway locations minutes from home. Whether a beach barge, a riverside pool, or a sandy street, these new spaces for recreation and leisure are novel interventions that make the urban environment a constant source of surprise and discovery. —ZR

roundtable discussion

paola antonelli
curator, department of architecture and design,
the museum of modern art and VAI trustee

deedee gordon
founder, look-look, los angeles

natalie jeremijenko
design engineer and techno-artist

anne pasternak
director, creative time

susan t. rodriguez
partner, polshek partnership and VAI trustee

dan wood
partner, WORK architecture company

*The following conversation took place in
spring 2005 at Van Alen Institute. This text is
an edited version of the original transcript.*

antonelli What makes a place fun? In some places,
it is driven by money, such as in Las Vegas or Dubai.
In other cities, it is art and architecture. In others,
it is sports and recreation.

jeremijenko I think it might be useful to look at how
fun is institutionalized in cities and the radically
different ideas of fun. There are the Las Vegas
and the Coney Island models based on vices and
frivolity. There are SeaWorld and Disneyland,
which are the 1950s institutionalized versions of
fun. There is a radically different version of fun that
is being institutionalized now which is much more
about health and leisure. Whereas the treadmill
was traditionally the icon of health, now it is much
more about being in functioning urban ecosystems
or near the waterfront in cities.

pasternak When I think about fun and cities, I think
of traditional health and recreation models. While
it's great to jog or rollerblade along a park path,
or play basketball or handball, it is not everybody's
idea of fun. While I think we should have more
healthy recreational opportunities in our cities,
I'd like to see a greater variety.

antonelli In 1969, the administration called
New York "the Fun City". A few years later, New
York was desperate and bankrupt. There was
a campaign to bring tourists back to Broadway.
Does real fun always entail a little risk?

pasternak Coney Island is fun because it has a
real edge; it's actually quite seedy. It's not the kind
of New York that you experience on an everyday
basis. The most fun I had in our city in recent years
was when I went to a New York Yankees game.
I just loved screaming out loud in public. I was
shocked by the extent of my own pleasure. We do
not have many opportunities to be totally free to
express and enjoy ourselves.

wood Parkour is very interesting, and is a
non-prescribed activity that is fun. The inventor
of Parkour was David Belle, who stars in the
film *District 13* that came out in 2004. It fuses
dance, skateboarding, and athletics. It is about

experiencing the city by moving through it using your body. The participants get from one place to another by traversing the urban fabric in the most beautiful and most acrobatic way possible.

pasternak There is special footwear for these people, with little metal plates on the bottom of the soles that make it easier to grind down rails and ride through the city's variable surfaces freely. Urban Climbers are another group that finds ways to use the city in risky, creative, and even illegal ways as they climb over buildings the same way in which they would climb over mountains. I love these kinds of individual actions, because they keep our experience of the city surprising and claim our public spaces for creative individuality.

This is harder to maintain as our city operates with an increased level of paranoia. For example, twenty years ago, Creative Time presented a project called *The National Monument to Freedom of Expression*. In essence, the piece is a huge red megaphone that amplifies the remarks of anyone who speaks into it. We represented this piece during the last Presidential election season in 2004. Though I love to scream out loud in public venues like baseball stadiums, others feel differently, as we learned from the many people who were fearful of speaking into the megaphone. They were afraid their voices were being recorded by the FBI. The fear of expressing oneself, vocally or otherwise, in public spaces is a clear result of the culture of fear in which we now live, and the accompanying heightened security around us. It's something that has to be addressed when thinking about having or creating fun in the public realm of the city.

antonelli DeeDee, what's your experience with younger people? Where do they get their fun?

gordon They do a lot in the privacy of their own homes. Technology allows young people to customize all of their experiences while they sit in their bedrooms.

antonelli So their public spaces are on the computer?

gordon Exactly. They can interact with whomever they want. They can customize all of their communication. They can decide which blogs they want to look at. They can decide which podcasts they want to listen to. They can have multiple identities and networking groups. However, young people also live a mobile lifestyle. Their mission control can be taken wherever they go via a laptop, their iPod, or PDA. There is a certain safety in that space; they do not have to deal with the security at the mall breathing down their neck.

jeremijenko I think that this is why, for example, young Japanese girls really took to cell phones more than any other community; they have no other public spaces. They are not allowed to gather in public space. I think that the real problem is a growing mentality that all young people are nuisances. We are prohibiting them from public space.

antonelli Do our cities provide any spaces that are actually fun for young people?

gordon Most of the spaces are made by large corporations. For example, in a city like Tokyo, the spaces for young people are big arcades or man-made complexes where you can surf and ski in the same dome.

rodriguez And yet when we think of Central Park and the popularity of the concerts and theater performances that are organized there and art projects such as Christo and Jeanne-Claude's *The Gates*, for example, it illustrates that people love coming together in public spaces. Whether you were a fan of *The Gates* or not, the one thing that I think everybody agreed upon was that people wanted to come together and have a memorable and collective experience.

jeremijenko In San Francisco, one of the biggest attractions is Pier 39. People crowd there to look at the seals. I think the challenge of the 21st century is how to make play that is consequential, generative, productive, and perhaps even remediative.

gordon Participation is key for young people. They want to be involved. We do a lot of work with Fortune 500 companies and get young people involved in the design of marketing campaigns. They really love it because someone is taking them seriously. I have a magazine called *Look-Look* that comes out twice a year and features photos, writing, drawings, and other art by young people between the ages of 14 and 30. Recently, we put out a call for artwork via our website. Without any additional marketing, I received submissions from young people from 29 countries. I think it worked because there were no limitations as to who could be involved and what people could send.

jeremijenko There is a difference, however, between open systems and free-for-alls. Structuring participation is what designers can do. For example, an experiment that I have found to be very successful in engaging a peer group in social activities is the Robot Dog project. It is an open source robotics project. We take commercially available robotic dog toys and upgrade them mechanically and electronically. We give them a new nose, which is an environmental toxin center, and a new brain that tells the dogs to sniff out environmental toxins. Instead of barking the National Anthem or walking in circles, we adapt them, upgrade them, and release them as packs. Ten kids did this recently with me on the Mission Bay landfill site right next door to SeaWorld. We released five dogs. Eight news cameras swarmed the site to watch the robotic dogs sniff out environmental toxins. City Council members and representatives from the mayor's office were there. It was fascinating for the kids to participate in something that was engaging the city. We also tested the dogs in the Bronx with kids from a local high school. The kids had never done any programming or engineering but they really got into the project and were interviewed on television about the site and its interest to the community. This project encouraged them to be active citizens.

pasternak I think this partially illustrates that people can have "fun" when they are engaged with the purpose of the work they are doing and when they take interest in the place in which they live. Games have become a popular way of investigating places thanks to flashmobs and artists Blast Theory and Glowlab.

wood I think something is fun only when it is a unique experience. When something starts to be duplicated and you understand the end result, it is no longer fun. A game is no longer fun when you have mastered it. I think that is also the same for eco-tourism. It starts out as fun for the surfers and backpackers but by the time it gets developed and commercialized it is no longer as exciting or as much fun.

pasternak There is fun in doing something you are not supposed to do. There is a thrill in breaking rules. The joy of taking something that is scripted, like city streets, and seeing how you can mess with their rules on your own terms can be exciting.

antonelli Let's think of a model of fun that requires neither money nor a particular set of circumstances. It is not easy. But there are some objects that act as catalysts and provoke chain reactions. The soccer ball is one of these. Perhaps, in the United States, it is the basketball.

wood If you go to Flushing Meadows Corona Park in Queens, where a lot of immigrant groups live, the weekends are dominated by soccer games. People from different countries team up and play against each other. Soccer really brings people from different cultures together and is fascinating in that respect.

gordon We just did a global study with young men between the ages of 19 and 24. Soccer was one of the number one things they mentioned that made them feel part of a community.

antonelli To return to what makes a place fun, I think that to go to a place that you have never been to before is fun. Cities that continue to be an enormous surprise for me include Jerusalem, Hong Kong, Tokyo, New York, and Los Angeles.

pasternak Governors Island is a special place and until recently no one had access to it. It is a former Coast Guard base. There are historic forts, mansions, a bowling alley, a swimming pool, a dance hall, and a hospital that is clearly haunted. Governors Island was abandoned, so when you go there it feels a bit like a ghost town or a historic recreation site with a past you can really feel. It is beautiful and ripe with potential, but there's something wonderfully odd and perverse about its current state. People should visit it before it is developed and loses its current qualities.

wood One of the attractions of cities is their unnaturalness.

rodriguez I think the density of cities is fun. It is totally engaging and overwhelming.

pasternak The sensory overload, with its color, sound, and velocity, can be exhilarating as much as it can induce panic, nausea, and anger.

wood The unexpected object or activity in cities is fun.

antonelli My idea of fun is not very adrenaline-inducing. It is riding on a public bus, not a tourist bus, and looking out onto a city that I do not know.

gordon I have to admit that being in New York and listening to other people's conversations on the subway is fun.

pasternak Sound is really overlooked in urban design, yet it has a tremendous influence on an environment. We have developed a number of sound-based art projects at the base of the Brooklyn Bridge, at the World Financial Center, and on the riverfront. One project that I especially love was by artist Nina Katchadourian, sponsored by SculptureCenter. She rewired a whole bunch of car alarms in New York with bird sounds. When

the alarms were triggered, people heard the chirping of birds rather than the blare of sirens. It was fun, imaginative, and humane.

antonelli What do we think of Times Square?

pasternak Fun.

antonelli Still fun to me, too.

rodriguez It is not fun to work there because it is always really congested but it is fun to be in Times Square if you do not have an agenda.

antonelli It will be fun when the design for the TKTS cut-price theater tickets booth is constructed in Times Square. Van Alen Institute ran the competition for a new design in 1997 and it was recently announced that enough money has been raised to finally do the project.

antonelli Going through Times Square in a cab at night is fun.

pasternak It is a stunning media-collaged environment. There are many ways to engage with it. It is open to interpretation—that is the key.

High Square

High Square was conceived by Julien De Smedt and Bjarke Ingels for a 32,000-square-foot public space elevated above the city on the roof of a department store in the heart of Copenhagen. De Smedt proposed the idea to Magasin Du Nord, one of Denmark's most famous department stores in summer 2002 and has since been working with the Municipality of Copenhagen and Realdania Research, a center for public space research, to realize the project. The design will give the city its first elevated public space with views stretching across the city and the harbor, as far away as Sweden. The design incorporates a landscaped terrace of multiple heights that spans across the entire roof of the shopping center with areas for sunbathing, theater and dance performances, outdoor film screenings, and visual arts projections. At the south end is an elevated area with a basketball court and sports field. A helipad is also included in the design.

High Square has been designed to be publicly accessible 24 hours a day via an escalator running up the side of the department store, as well as through the store, which has a direct connection at ground level to Copenhagen's subway system. In an effort to make further connections between the roof and the city streets, De Smedt and Ingels have proposed enlarging the existing rooftop public parking lot and integrating it into the scheme with an additional access way for buses and taxis to further encourage a flow of traffic that will enliven the space during the day and night.

De Smedt says that Copenhagen, which is currently best known for its historical architecture, "is a nostalgic image of the city that once was and does not reflect the city's current content, activities, desires, or demands...In order to prevent the inner cities from petrifying into well-kept museums of the past and to breathe life into the historical surroundings we need to invent new ways of sharing space." The design team conducted a series of interviews with people in Copenhagen to determine the types of programs that might be accommodated on the square. These programs include

a soccer pitch, lounge spaces, a film screening area, and viewing terraces. The project not only aims to create an innovative new recreational destination four stories above ground but also to be a catalyst for further change in the city. "The square is our stand against the privatization of public space in the city," asserts De Smedt. "It is an example of how space might be given back to the city." It is hoped that the square will encourage new activities and uses to emerge in nearby areas of the city, stimulating development in spaces such as the adjacent Flower Square, a public plaza that stretches in front of the shopping center. The project is part of a larger consolidated effort on the part of local architects to create an updated and forward-looking identity for Copenhagen through the transformation of its public spaces. —ZR

1 Aerial view of High Square in Copenhagen
2 Elevation of High Square from street level
3, 4 Activity zones on High Square
5 High Square in winter
6 Outdoor film screening

55

2

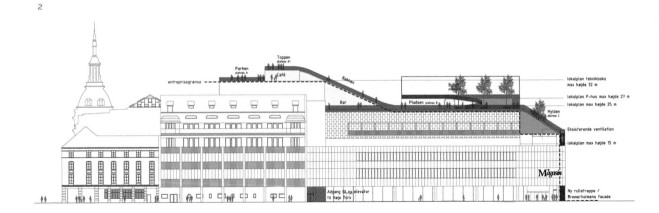

Tokachi Ecology Park   Takano Landscape Planning Company   Obihiro City, Japan   2006

Since establishing his firm in 1973, Fumiaki Takano has made a name for himself developing master plans and designs for large-scale parks focused on community involvement and child development. He is perhaps most well-known for designing the Children's Forest at Showa Kinen Park, completed in 1992 on the site of a former U.S. military base in Tachikawa, on the outskirts of Tokyo. This project was the testing ground for some of Takano's most innovative play space designs, including those of the recently opened Tokachi Ecology Park in Hokkaido. Takano notes that his designs aim "for a symbiosis of man and nature," and this is reflected in the diverse program of play features integrated into the parklands.

Tokachi Ecology Park covers 350 acres around the Tokachi River in Hokkaido prefecture, northern Japan. Located three miles from the center of Obihiro, the park serves a population of 380,000. The park's play spaces educate children about the local river ecosystem while also encouraging children to explore the landscape directly. "As children's lives have become more structured in response to the demands of a competitive educational system, time for play has shrunk." Takano's design for Tokachi aims to give children access to nature, wildlife, and open spaces, inviting physical activity, creativity, and discovery.

For all of his park designs, Takano commissions new equipment from a team of collaborators who have been working with him since the 1970s. The Bouncing Dome is an air-filled canvas structure invented by Jiro Takahashi. The inflated dome, resembling a small hill, is situated in a slightly sunken area of the park, surrounded by trees and hills. The dome vibrates as people move across it and offers the feeling of weightlessness, allowing children to jump, spin, roll, and tumble freely. Takano organized numerous community meetings and workshops to solicit ideas for their designs. The Bouncing Dome is a favorite component of their parks because it is accessible to all children and adults, including those with disabilities.

Future plans for Tokachi Ecology Park include a fog and water environment that changes constantly depending on the weather conditions. In the original Fog Forest for Showa Kinen Park by artist Fujiko Nakaya, an adjustable pump pressurizes water through hundreds of vapor nozzles, resulting in a variable flow of mist across the park. The wind filters the fog across the landscape, creating blankets of clouds that grow denser in places, covering children until they disappear, and then dispersing to reveal them. Takano explains that the fog and water "make us feel our environment." Net play equipment is also planned for the park. The Rainbow Hammock at Showa Kinen Park, designed by Toshiko Horiuchi MacAdam, consists of a set of 60 multicolored net structures, offering a far more complex set of physical conditions than possible with conventional play equipment. Committed to preserving and protecting nature, Takano believes that it is essential for children to have physical contact with their surroundings. His projects also illustrate the potential for human development through play. —ZR

1, 4 Bouncing Dome in Tokachi Ecology Park, Obihiro City, Japan
2 Net play equipment in Children's Forest,
Showa Kinen Park, Tachikawa, Japan
3, 5 Fog environment, Children's Forest, Showa Kinen Park

3

5

Skatepark

Acconci Studio

San Juan, Puerto Rico

2008

In 2003, Acconci Studio was invited by Public Art Projects of Puerto Rico to design a skateboard park in San Juan. The new park is part of Governor Sila Marí Calderón's $15 million project for more than 100 new public works for the capital city. The 30,000-square-foot skate park is located in Third Millennium Park, situated in Isla Verde, to the north of the city. Acconci Studio took the topography of the existing parkland—a pedestrian bridge over a restaurant, a conical hill, and a slope leading to a plateau at the edge of the Atlantic Ocean—as a starting point for their design. "We wanted our skatepark to make use of the views across the ocean and the three points across the site. We proceeded as if the skatepark was already there; all we had to do

was fit out the high points so that they could function as a skatepark," notes Vito Acconci.

For the park, Acconci Studio drew on their concept for a skateboard park in Avignon, France. They took this research many steps further and consulted with skateboarders, developed computer and scale models, and collaborated with skatepark builders Wormhoudt, located in Santa Cruz, to determine the design of the park. The design team wanted to integrate pedestrians and onlookers into the skatepark so they built the park from three reinforced concrete ramps, the outer two for skateboarders and the inner ramp for pedestrians who can survey the action on both sides. The ramps weave in and out and up and under each other creating a complex

network of spaces. The skateboarding ramps go through the conical hill opening up to form skateboard bowls inside for more advanced skating. Parts of the ramps are enclosed and parts are left open to views across the landscape. Lit from within, the ramps glow from outside encouraging passersby to peek inside. This is no mere gimmick for Acconci Studio's skateboard park. It is truly a performance space that makes room for the non-skateboarding spectator. —ZR

1 Stepped ramps at the skatepark, San Juan, Puerto Rico
2 Skating bowls within the conical hill
3 Half-pipe ramps leading to the ocean
4 Half-pipe ramps extending from the plateau

Floating Swimming Pool

Jonathan Kirschenfeld Associates · Brooklyn, New York · 2007

From the 1870s to the 1940s, as many as fifteen floating river bathhouses stationed at various points off the coast of Manhattan offered residents the chance to swim in what was then relatively unpolluted river water. Jonathan Kirschenfeld Associates' design for the Floating Swimming Pool recalls the program and entry sequence of the 19th-century floating bathhouse: visitors enter from the shore via a gangway, passing through an arrival porch to a central raised courtyard, around which locker rooms, showers, and a snack bar are situated.
From the locker rooms, visitors follow a ramp down to the pool deck, catching views of the skyline and river along the way. The contemporary pool has been adapted from a former industrial barge, with modern elec-trical, waste treatment, and water systems, but it will once again afford New Yorkers the opportunity to reconnect with the city's surrounding waterways, as well as provide

a much-needed, modern public swimming pool. —EY

1 Deck of Floating
Swimming Pool,
Brooklyn, New York

2 Model of Floating
Swimming Pool,
Brooklyn, New York

Spree Bridge Bathing Ship

AMP arquitectos with
Gil Wilk and Susanne Lorenz · Berlin, Germany · 2004

In 2002, Berlin's public art association, Stadtkunstprojekte e.V., held a comp-etition to generate ideas to link the city to the Spree River through public art projects on and around existing bridges. Tenerife's AMP arquitectos teamed up with Berlin-based architect Gil Wilk and artist Susanne Lorenz to reinterpret this idea, designing a new "bridge to the Spree" by reusing a former shipping barge as a modern-day urban marine bath. Recalling the 19th-century tradition of the floating river bathhouse, the team modified the 30-year-old barge with coated film and pool floodlights. Since 2005, when Gil Wilk and architect Thomas Freiwald added an air-filled, plastic "membrane" to enclose the pool and deck areas, the Bathing Ship has been open year-round as a sauna and lounge with panoramic views of the river. —EY

1 Aerial view of Summer
Bathing Ship, Berlin,
Germany

2 Winter
Bathing Ship

Harbor Bath

PLOT = JDS + B.I.G.   Copenhagen, Denmark   2003

Copenhagen's first floating harbor bath in 50 years, the Harbor Bath opened to the public in June 2003 as part of the city government's ambitious plan to transform Copenhagen's industrial inner harbor into a cleaner and more environmentally friendly mixed-use district. Since the late 1980s, the city government has led an initiative to limit commercial shipping traffic in the inner harbor, to relocate factories away from the water, and to reduce the amount of wastewater entering the harbor through storm-water overflows. At the same time, developers and planners have teamed up to revitalize Islands Brygge, a formerly industrial district adjacent to the inner harbor, giving it new residential, cultural, and recreational functions. The Harbor Bath, situated along the old shipping dock in Islands Brygge, is in many ways the culmination of these efforts. It offers Copenhageners the opportunity to bathe in newly clean seawater while

also serving as a dynamic extension to the new Harbor Park.

Accommodating up to 600 people daily in a variety of different water and "land" environments, including a sloped wading pool, an angled diving platform, and a handicapped-accessible ramp, the 27,000-square-foot Harbor Bath functions more like an urban beach than a traditional swimming hall. The architects, PLOT = JDS + B.I.G., note that

the design consists of "reinterpreting the water...by adding land." In urban planning terms, the project is about re-envisioning a new public life for the harbor by shifting away from heavy industry and towards a more sustainable mixture of residential, cultural, and recreational uses. —EY

1 Aerial view of Harbor Bath, Copenhagen, Denmark

Vinaròs Urban Beach

Guallart Architects   Vinaròs, Spain   2008

As part of a larger regeneration scheme aimed at reconnecting the seaside city of Vinaròs, Spain, to the waterfront, Guallart Architects has been working to develop a series of public spaces, and most notably, small public beaches.

The beachscapes are made from a multi-leveled configuration of wooden platforms that are overlaid over the existing headland. The platforms are constructed in a hexagonal pattern so that they can adapt to the irregular and

rocky terrain and allow users to enjoy the coastline. Guallart also proposes tethering an artificial wooden island to the beach during the summer. —ZR

1 Vinaròs Urban Beach, Vinaròs, Spain

Urban Beaches

Paris, Amsterdam, Brussels, Rome

For the past five years, during July and August, Mayor Bertrand Delanoë has hired scenographer Jean-Christophe Choblet to "stage" a beach reminiscent of a different sunny locale by towing in tons of sand, beach umbrellas, "parabrume" fog machines, lounge chairs, and palm trees to the center of Paris. Closing off a two-mile section of the Georges Pompidou expressway, a major highway built in the 1960s along the Right Bank, Paris Plage opens up the riverside to pedestrians, rollerbladers, sunbathers, and street performers. In past years there have been stations along the beach devoted to specific leisure activities, such as rock climbing, beach volleyball, and golf, as well as a concert series and evening film projections. Intended to benefit families that lack the time or resources to travel to an actual beach during the summer holidays, Paris Plage has become so popular that it is now a tourist attraction in its own right, providing public space for relaxation and play for both residents and visitors during a time when most of the city is closed for the summer.

The success of Paris Plage has inspired other European cities, such as Amsterdam, Berlin, Brussels, Budapest, and Rome to set up similar "beach atmospheres" along their own waterfronts during the summer months. In Amsterdam, the municipality works together with individual districts to organize public parties, film screenings, games, and concerts in a number of improvised "beach" locations. In Brussels, the city sponsors Bruxelles Les Bains, a month-long summer festival offering a host of beach-related activities along the canal. While swimming in the canal is still strictly forbidden, visitors can participate in yoga, taste gourmet foods, play beach sports, or receive a massage by the edge of the water. In Rome, the beach-themed Tiber Village has helped spruce up the banks of the Tiber River, replacing the weeds and trash with swimming pools, cafés, and beach umbrellas during the summer. —EY

1 Paris Plage, Paris, France (2005) 2 Tiber Village, Rome, Italy (2005) 3 Amsterdam Plage, Amsterdam, the Netherlands (2005) 4 Bruxelles Les Bains, Brussels, Belgium (2004)

Haggerston Playground — erect architecture and Sarah Lewison — London, United Kingdom — 2005

Erect architecture's design ethos strives for a rare blend of innovative design, environmental sensitivity, and community outreach. As architects Barbara Kaucky and Susanne Tutsch write, "we enjoy stretching our brains for apt responses to social, ecological and all other challenges." The Haggerston Playground in Hackney, East London, combines this thoughtful approach with an extensive effort in community consultation. When Surestart commissioned erect architecture to design the new playground, the architects organized a series of meetings with local parents and led a design workshop at a local primary school, in which kids built their own "dream play landscapes" out of playdough. These discussions inspired a rolling landscape of grassy ridges and integrated custom play equipment. While the variable topography helps separate different functional zones and age groups, it also heightens the children's sense of perception and

discovery. Sustainable wood play equipment is embedded into the mini hills and valleys, helping children explore the terrain, and other natural materials such as fragrant herbs, playbark, and compacted gravel are used throughout. —EY

1 Haggerston Playground, London, United Kingdom

Grounds for Play — Gareth Hoskins Architects — Glasgow, United Kingdom — 2004

In 2001, the House for an Art Lover, designed by Charles Rennie Mackintosh in 1901, partnered with Glasgow City Council to invite architects and artists to submit ideas for developing the adjacent park into a playground. Glasgow-based Gareth Hoskins Architects won the competition with the scheme, Grounds for Play, a lush, undulating landscape of convex, concave, and flat elliptical islands.

Scattered around the park grounds "like fallen petals upon a lawn," the ellipses create curved paths for children to run around and a fluid structure into which play objects, such as an elevated copper "cloud," which functions as both a tunnel and a slide, and a set of pastel fiberglass garden seats called "jelly babies," are inserted. —EY

1 Grounds for Play, Glasgow, United Kingdom

Geo Play Public Playground — SonArc — Long Island City, New York — 2007

Geo Play is a highly interactive public playground designed to encourage children to play with sound and develop curiosity about other cultures. Situated on a world map, the playground features four types of play equipment centered on the themes of water, the seven continents, music, and science. Playground designers SonArc created several different interactive "boats," one of which, the SS Jules Verne, evokes a Viking ship and features tubular oars that play sound when tapped or spoken into. On each of the continents, SonArc has developed a series of abstract, acoustic sculptures where children can recreate sounds reminiscent of the music played there. On the Indonesian archipelago, for instance, children can play a set of gongs similar to those used in gamelan performances. —EY

1 Geo Play Public Playground, Long Island City, NY

Recreational Ground   Heatherwick Studio   Wanchai, Hong Kong   2010

For the past several years, the local government of one of Hong Kong's busiest and oldest commercial districts, Wanchai, has led a major effort to regenerate some of the area's outdated public spaces. Following a conference in 2001, the British Council Hong Kong and the Wanchai District Council invited London-based designer and artist Thomas Heatherwick to redesign the Southorn Recreational Ground, a park that since 1929 has supported a variety of community activities—from colorful street performances, to community festivals, a night market, Chinese chess games, and soccer matches.

Heatherwick's redesign takes into account the ground's traditional identity as a multifunctional gathering place and responds to the community's needs for additional green space, more room for play and seating, and an inviting atmosphere for all users. The ground is divided into several distinct layers: the lowered soccer pitch, the new green area, and the "floating" basketball

courts. By lowering the existing pitch by five feet and adding a translucent, elevated platform of basketball courts 26 feet above it, the design opens up over 23,000 square feet of green space on the ground's southwest edge. This new green area features 50 large trees for shade and a 1,300-foot ribbon

of sculptural stone, which integrates seating, lighting, gates, and planters in a single, fluid element. —EY

1 Southorn Recreational Ground, Wanchai, Hong Kong

2 Elevated basketball courts 3 Lowered soccer pitch

Westblaak Skatepark   Dirk van Peijpe (dS+V Rotterdam)   Rotterdam, the Netherlands   2001

By moving through public space, performing, and experimenting, skateboarders appropriate the city itself as a giant playground. Unfortunately, despite this playful attitude, skaters are often judged a nuisance and relegated to the outskirts of towns. In Rotterdam, a group of skateboarders grew tired of constantly being banished from the city center and drafted a petition which they presented to the municipal

government. The city responded positively to their initiative by creating a huge outdoor skatepark in the empty middle section of the Westblaak boulevard. Now the largest skatepark in the Netherlands, Westblaak Skatepark covers 72,000 square feet, featuring eleven silver skateboarding obstacles and a beginners' track. —EY

1 Overall view of Westblaak Skatepark, Rotterdam

Sports Pavilion   Ábalos & Herreros   Madrid, Spain   2003

In 1999, Madrid's municipal government commissioned Ábalos & Herreros to design a public sports pavilion in the midst of the lush and historic El Retiro Park. Serving park visitors, local schools, sports teams, and residents of the dense Retiro neighborhood, the 7,000-square-foot pavilion is a hybrid space both programmatically and formally. A simple, half-submerged box accommodates a mixture of

recreational and support spaces. Standard materials were employed throughout the building, such as wire mesh for the façade, which doubles as a structure for climbing plants. From afar, the pavilion appears as an abstract, immaterial version of the 17th-century topiary, similar to those that line the park's gardens and pathways. —EY

1 Sports Pavilion in El Retiro Park, Madrid, Spain

The Garden of Knowledge   Monika Gora   Malmö, Sweden   2001

Designed by landscape architect and artist Monika Gora, the Garden of Knowledge is a 21,000-square-foot public park to the east of Santiago Calatrava's Turning Torso tower in Malmö. In contrast to the orderly high-tech atmosphere of the surrounding development, the Garden is a disjointed labyrinth of poetically themed spaces, divided by plain pinewood partitions and incorporating familiar raw materials. Visitors enter along an asphalt path, encountering a series of scripted spaces reminiscent of a children's playground: a closet with a large, overflowing toilet; and timber rooms filled with live geese, stones, a pine tree, and an oversized garden. Once outside the park, visitors can climb up into a straw-covered "castle in the air" and survey the entire scene from above. From there, it is clear that the Garden of Knowledge looks to question the concepts we have developed to systematize and control the world—"order," "civilization," "sustainability"—

in favor of basic human senses and emotions. —EY

1 Entrance to the Garden of Knowledge, Malmö, Sweden
2 "Castles in the Air" overlooking the Garden
3 Detail of the Garden

Tentstation   büro für planung + raum/berlin   Berlin, Germany   2006

This summer, Berlin's old Poststadion sports complex hosts a new leisure activity—urban camping. Tentstation, an urban campsite for up to 150 tents, was conceived as a fun, centrally located, and inexpensive lodging option for visitors to the 2006 World Cup. From May to September, visitors can rent a tent or bring their own, staying on the verdant grounds surrounding the complex's former outdoor swimming

pool, originally built in the 1950s and now renovated to feature new lighting, stairs, and a sand layer at the bottom

to accommodate beach sports. —EY

1 Tentstation, Berlin, Germany

Balham Community Space   Lynch Architects   London, United Kingdom   2005

In 2003, the Balham Town Centre Partnership and the Artmarkit artist collective enlisted Balham residents Patrick and Claudia Lynch to redesign a neglected triangle of land in the town center adjacent to a supermarket and a large parking lot. The 3,700-square-foot site has since been transformed from a transitional, littered, and rodent-infested space into an intimate public piazza. Lynch Architects abstracted the traditional metal railing motif to

form an angular canopy over the space. Rather than acting as a boundary, the railing now guides people into the piazza through an archway. Benches, landscaping, lighting, and a secure power source have also been installed, allowing the space to host a variety of activities, including the Balham Festival and a wintertime ice rink. —EY

1 Climbing wall in Balham Community

Space, London, United Kingdom

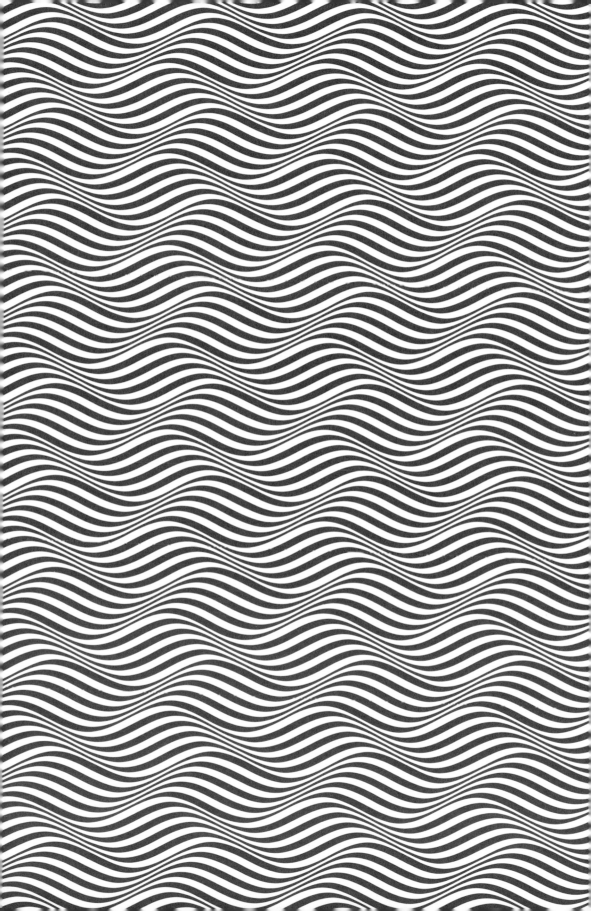

the connected city

The built form of the city dominates our understanding of the architecture of urban environments and yet the routes between buildings are more than just a transportation network from one place to another. City streets, cycle paths, trails, greenways, promenades, and highways, both virtual and real, are spaces that are constantly in flux. Energized by movement, they are places where paths cross, the mixing of activities and people occur, connections are made, and exchange happens. Whether full of slow spaces or fast networks, *The Connected City* fosters a diversity of activities and social inter-actions, linking people and places in physical and virtual locations.

These ideas are at the heart of the projects presented here. A new parkland located in an impoverished neighborhood in Rio de Janeiro is being implemented in an effort to encourage interaction between people from different backgrounds and economic spheres. In Seoul, New York, and Oakland, California, new connections are being made that link the city to the natural environment promoting new experiences and healthy excursions that contribute to the sustainability of the urban frame. Other projects explore how technological interventions, art projects, urban games, and happenings can create networked spaces that bring people together to share common experiences and allow access to information, both historical and contemporary. In London, a major new cultural development is experimenting with unprecedented forms of connectivity inspired by the ubiquity of mobile technology and wireless communication systems. In Southern Sudan, similar ideas are being transferred on a smaller scale as an immediate response to the current humanitarian crisis. The last assemblage of projects are urban explorations that take inspiration from the work of collectives such as the Situationist International, founded in 1957, and in operation in Europe through the 1960s. Using the city as a space for interrogation and provocation, these interventions open up the city and create a flow of people, commodities, and ideas. These projects illustrate that *The Connected City* is a place of chance encounters, unexpected discoveries, and social exchange where citizens are taken on a new journey time after time. —ZR

roundtable discussion

janet abrams
director, university of minnesota design institute,
co-editor of *else/where: mapping* and VAI trustee

benjamin aranda
partner, aranda/lasch and terraswarm

michael bierut
partner, pentagram

jane harrison
principal, ATOPIA and ATOPIA research

steven johnson
author, *everything bad is good for you:
how today's popular culture is actually making
us smarter* (2005) and *mind wide open: your brain
and the neuroscience of everyday life* (2003)

katie salen
director of graduate studies, design and
technology, parsons school of design
and co-author of *the game design reader*
(2005) and *rules of play: game design
fundamentals* (2004)

kevin slavin
co-founder and managing director, area/code

dana spiegel
executive director of NYCwireless
and an MIT media lab alumna

*The following conversation took place in
spring 2005 at Van Alen Institute. This text is
an edited version of the original transcript.*

abrams In 2002, the Design Institute began a multi-year research program on mapping in various design disciplines and dimensions, with the aim of finding fresh ways to think about the city and exploring how digital communication technologies might enable new experiences of the urban realm. We took as a premise the idea of the "City as Database" and started out by commissioning nine teams to create alternative cartographies of Minneapolis and St. Paul, in Minnesota. We also decided to map the city physically, through an urban game. In late 2002, I commissioned Katie Salen, Frank Lantz, and Nick Fortuno, working together as Playground, to develop a game. We launched it as the "Big Urban Game," or "B.U.G.," that September. The notion was that the city is a ready-made game board: you just need to enlarge the pieces, and have portable "squares" for them to land on at designated sites around the city.

In essence, the B.U.G. was a five-day race between three giant inflatable game pieces, traveling along three different routes, between daily checkpoints, towards a single destination; the piece that reached the final stop in the shortest cumulative time was the winner. The game pieces were physically carried between checkpoints by teams of students and volunteers. The general public was invited to determine which of two possible routes their team's piece should travel, by casting a daily vote on a special section of our website. By the fifth day, more than 3,300 people had registered online to take part in the game.

harrison What was the goal of the game?

abrams To encourage people to take note of and think about their urban environment, and at a broader level, to create a lively social experience that could serve as a metaphor for collective decision-making in the urban environment.

harrison How did you develop the concept Katie?

salen We tried to come up with something that everybody in the Twin Cities could immediately relate to. We wanted to create a game that any-body could play. We realized that one thing that everyone shared was the knowledge of how to get around their city. As a result, we determined that the game would be based on an understanding of the city traffic patterns. Each day, players chose from a set of possible routes that would allow their team's game piece to move fastest through the city. Some of the routes were significantly longer than others but the shorter routes had more obstacles, such as a lot of traffic. The most successful players were those that knew the city best.

abrams Michael, you worked on an interesting project recently to do with the taxi? How did that come about?

bierut It was a project organized with Parsons School of Design and Project for Public Spaces. It began with a series of workshops that explored the design of the New York City taxi and how it functions. What struck me in the presentations was how ubiquitous taxis are and how dominant they are in the urban streetscape. When you ask someone what they think of a New York City taxi, the image in a lot of people's minds is an image that is no longer germane. A lot of people talk about the Checker Cab, which no longer exists. It was a bespoke creation manufactured in the early 1920s only to function as a New York City taxi. Today, the bland Ford Crown Victoria serves as the chassis for the New York City taxi. This car is not looked on with much affection by anyone and is actually dysfunctional in terms of the footprint it occupies and the amount of gas it uses per mile. Our goal was twofold: we wanted to make some functional improvements on the taxi while reinvigorating it as an icon. Before the workshop, Project for Public Spaces had taken a poll about what users liked and disliked about New York City taxis. Most of the dislikes had nothing to do with the amount of leg room or the actual cab. Instead, they had to do with the perceived shortcoming of the drivers. Just like the Checker Cab had an iconography we held on to, I think there is an archetypal New York City cab driver that we all know from screwball comedies from the 1930s and 1940s; a wisecracking guy from the Bronx or Brooklyn, chomping on a cigar, dispensing street-smart wisdom. However, today

98% of cab drivers are immigrants to the United States. They may be wisecracking, they may be street-smart, but they are not likely to be natives, at least not of the Bronx, Brooklyn, or anywhere else in the United States.

Our goal was to find ways to break down the divisions between the cab driver and the passenger.

harrison I think that the notion of the city as a playground or as a gameboard is useful here. In 1996, my partner and I guest-edited an issue of *Architectural Design* on "Games of Architecture." In retrospect for ATOPIA, this was the beginning of our engagement with what we call Relational Architecture, working specifically with the structural, material, and technological possibilities of interactive play as an activity, and as a metaphor, connecting people, places, and things. The taxi driver-passenger relationship can be more affecting, and in a sense more useful if driver-to-driver and passenger-to-driver exchanges are encouraged, enriched, and most importantly, enjoyed—if the incredibly intricate global knowledge base that you are suggesting exists, is captured.

bierut Yes, by doing simple things. You could, for instance, list on the taxi driver's license located in the cab their place of birth or homeland, so it reads something like so and so from Senegal. Another idea is to periodically release a CD of music compiled by taxi drivers that passengers would have the option to listen to and purchase while traveling in a taxi. It would be an amazing compilation. People would love it. The HBO series "Taxicab Confessions" is really successful. Your idea would probably work because the very structure of the taxi works essentially as a confessional.

harrison But the confessional is only one of many possible spatial metaphors that define the experience of riding in a taxi cab, it is also a mobile ring-side seat for watching the city, occasionally a temporary retreat, or even a prison. The cell phone or any mobile communications device changes the space of the taxi cab by connecting it outwards to anywhere and anybody. This transforms the driver into a mobile dispatcher, a key player in a network that organizes the flow of people around the city. The passenger can be "virtually" at home, in the office, shopping, out with friends, or equally just another link in the network. The design opportunities here would include the redesign of the network, the taxi cab, the passenger's area, the driver's space, their seat, their clothes, their tools of communication.

spiegel I think that providing a connection between the passenger and the driver is really important, People who know nothing about each other are more willing to communicate if they have some common ground between them.

salen I think the invention of the cell phone is interesting to talk about in relation to taxi drivers. Cabbies were the biggest adopters of cell phones when they first came out because of the offer of free nights and weekends. This enabled them to be on the phone and connected to their fellow taxi drivers or family at home while they worked.

abrams Can these abstract networks be turned into something more tangible and accessible by people outside of these tight groups?

johnson The most interesting thing that could happen with technologies such as GPS systems is the integration of local knowledge. It comes under the idea of geo-tagging. Instead of tagging things with HTML you are tagging information using physical coordinates in space. You could start to get a sort of local blog with information about a corner of a city or a small section of a neighborhood where a new restaurant or a playground has just opened up, for example. You would anchor the information somehow in physical space so as you move through the city people could access it via their phone or PDA.

abrams But is it just about more applications and more toys—more projects that live within a certain sphere of culture, namely, the experimental underground? How do these projects cross over into the mainstream? Do these ideas set the rules

around which architects and designers are creating public spaces?

spiegel This is something NYCwireless is working on. We create hot spots in specific local spaces that can contain and help develop local knowledge about a particular area. Some of our hot spots have message boards about the surrounding couple of blocks.

abrams Who selects that information?

spiegel Residents or people who frequent the area.

aranda All of these technologies are protocols that merge with each other and set up an operational grid. Yet, I am always looking for ways out of these kinds of grids. It's clear these communication technologies continually redefine the tools of design but their disappointing indoctrination into our lifestyles through advertising and branding tends to smooth out the edges, hiding what might be a real discovery. At our office, we spent time trying to fray these edges in the skies over Brooklyn by attaching cameras onto trained pigeons flying in large flocks. We didn't know what kind of footage we'd get back but we didn't care so much; the project was both a way to see the city through a highly dynamic vantage point and also a way to position these imaging technologies (aerial footage) outside the standard grid of protocols usually associated with it (GIS or otherwise). In other words, when you're off the grid, there are other issues besides technology's fulfillment that come to the foreground. These issues are vital to design.

johnson I think I am becoming more optimistic about these types of systems. They are very web-like in the sense that they really only need one standardized definition, just as the web really only needs one standardized definition of what a URL is. What we now need are ways to define X and Y in physical space. Then you can let everything else be as fuzzy and open-ended and user-generated and undefined as you want it to be, as long as you have some standardized way of saying this is this point in physical space.

abrams Who is choosing the protocol by which something is gridded and mapped out?

johnson Basic cartography is as literal as talking about a central point in space. Human progress is always based on someone for some reason deciding that for some purpose—often to make money—that they are going to set up a series of systems, which eventually get out of control. Just think of blogging. You can now get insights into worlds that would be completely opaque to you, whether it is a blog that is run by a London Saville Row tailor or a Los Angeles porn producer.

spiegel I am very curious about how architects perceive the integration of architecture and technology in the built environment.

harrison We are addressing these issues with the Battersea Power Station project we're working on in London. Ultimately, if all goes well, the 36-acre site could be the largest integrated interactive media environment in Europe. We are working out how new communication technologies transform the way we design the physical environment— the architecture of form, material, light, and space— so that the interrelationship between the actual and virtual environments can be exploited, made more extreme, or their differences dissolved. Rather than calling ourselves architects, we describe our work as design, communications, and urbanism. Architecture is the practice of designing modes of operation. We are developing ways of practicing architecture that exploit and thrive on the often impossible realities of the global economy, cultural production, and political friction.

salen The problem I see with a lot of current mobile applications is that they only engage virtual space; they do not begin to identify or explore the interface between virtual space and real physical space. In addition, so far technology has really only been a catalyst for person-to-person contact, when that person is not in the same location as you. I was just at a conference that focused exclusively on location-based gaming. It was taken as a given at the conference that location meant geography

and GIS data. There are more interesting ways to think about how we define the concept of location. Location can be defined in relation to flows of activity, for example, or with regard to memory or perception of place. Some of the work the Alternate Reality Gaming community has been doing around this idea is really interesting. They are trying to explode distinctions between real and virtual place by challenging our notions of what "where" is through game play that takes place both on and off the screen.

abrams Kevin, what are some of the things you have been thinking about when designing games for public space?

slavin I have been thinking a lot about scalability and the notion of how to build tiny moments into games rather than always grand gestures. Traditionally, big games have been played in public space designed on a giant scale to affect huge numbers of people. However, in the continuum of our daily lives in public space, a 10-second experience has the possibility of transforming the entire day.

bierut I agree, and I think this idea ties in to what we have been speaking about. Powerful interventions, whether that means a CD of music produced by a taxi driver that the public has access to, a game in a public space, or a technological system that helps you tap into new experiences, help us see things differently and take note of our surroundings. They encourage us to build connections with the people and places around us. I think that idea is something genuine and worth pursuing.

Metropolitan Park

Jorge Mario Jáuregui   Rio de Janeiro, Brazil   2005

For more than ten years, Brazilian architect Jorge Mario Jáuregui has been working on projects in Rio de Janeiro's favela (shantytown) communities as part of the "Favela-Bairro Program." The scheme aims to promote the integration of the favelas with the rest of the city. The program will not only develop the infrastructure to bring roads, clean water, sewage systems, medical care, and other basic services to these neighborhoods; it will also facilitate the community interactions and participation needed to maintain such provisions. Jáuregui's latest project, the Manguinhos Complex, is a plan for urban and social development in an area where 28,000 inhabitants live in ten favelas at the main northern access point to the city. In addition to the informal residences characteristic of favelas, industrial buildings, educational and research institutions, commercial areas, and a portion of the city's port are located in this area. The unplanned communities that have never been integrated into the

city's infrastructure are further divided from the rest of the city by a railway line. This will be elevated above ground to make way for the central focus of the project, Metropolitan Park. The hope is that this new urban space will provide linkages between the informal favela communities and the rest of the city.

The idea for the park was born out of a series of public hearings and meetings that were led by Jáuregui and a multidisciplinary team of architects, engineers, planners, sociologists, psychiatrists, educators, medical personnel, and social workers. These sessions engaged residents in thinking about their environment and their immediate needs. Rather than proposing the eradication of the existing neighborhoods or conventional assistance programs that have failed to work since they were implemented in the 1930s, the Favela-Bairro Program aims to generate vital and healthy communities through interventions that provide new opportunities for residents. As Jáuregui puts it, "Our projects

need to help diminish the ecologically passive character of the favelas through the articulation of physical (urban, infrastructural, and landscape improvements), ecological (mental, social, and environmental impacts), and safety considerations for citizens."

Metropolitan Park is structured to be accessible to a broad range of people of different age ranges and varying interests, and will accommodate both passive and active recreation, as well as cultural activities. It will also provide jobs for local families. The park's program aims to provide alternative activities and attractions to counter the heavy drug dealing in the area and to generate other means of promoting the local economy.

The one-mile-long park, still in the process of being approved by the city, is scheduled to be completed in the next five years. —ZR

1 Aerial view of Metropolitan Park, Rio de Janeiro, Brazil

2 Manguinhos Complex
3 Manguinhos within urban context
4 Metropolitan Park

1

2

Floating Park

IROJE KHM architects & planners   Seoul, Korea   2007

Floating Park is a hybrid structure consisting of three pedestrian bridges that tie together parts of the mountain range in Seoul's picturesque BukHanSan National Park. The bridges, designed by IROJE KHM architects & planners, were commissioned by the Sungbuk District Office to provide walkers with a continuous path from mountain to mountain, spanning areas previously only accessible by car.

The bridges do more than function as walkways from one point to another: they have been designed as elevated platforms with distinct areas carved into their surfaces for performances and gatherings.

One of the bridges, covering 1,200 square feet, consists of a twisted steel canopy that supports a wooden platform with seating and planters. Its lattice-work and organic shape were inspired by asymmetrical forms found in nature. Design Principal Hyo Man Kim hopes that the curving form will function as a "living landmark" in the landscape. Floating Park will also be illuminated at night, creating a festive event space within the larger park. —ZR

1, 2, 3 Floating Park, Seoul, Korea

The High Line

Field Operations & Diller Scofidio + Renfro   New York, New York   2008

In 1999, Robert Hammond and Joshua David founded Friends of the High Line (FHL), a non-profit lobbying and advocacy group, with a mission to save the 1.2-mile-long abandoned elevated freight rail line that runs through the West Side of Manhattan from demolition. Six years later, not only has the railroad been saved but construction has begun to transform what Amanda Burden, chair of the New York City Planning Commission calls "one of the most unique open spaces in the world," into an elevated park for the city. The design is being orchestrated by landscape architects Field Operations and architects Diller Scofidio + Renfro, horticulturalist Piet Oudolf, artist Olafur Eliasson, and structural engineers Buro Happold. Their plan for a new recreational space for the city treats as

its point of reference the existing structure and the many indigenous plants growing on its surface as its natural condition.

The High Line was constructed in 1934 to carry freight safely through the city avoiding the street traffic. The last train ran on the tracks in 1980 and they have since been left abandoned.

In 2001, FHL organized an ideas competition designed to get people talking about the potential of the High Line as a structure for reuse at a time when the fate of the High Line was still undecided. The competition received 720 entries from 36 countries and generated international interest in FHL's project. Their efforts were rewarded in 2003 when the City of New York rezoned the neighborhood around the High Line to make way for the transformation of the site

into a new elevated park as part of a larger commercial and residential development on the West Side of Manhattan. In July 2004, from seven short-listed teams, "Agri-Tecture," was selected as the winning project.

James Corner, principal of Field Operations, describes their vision as being "inspired by the melancholic 'found' beauty of the High Line, where nature has reclaimed the once-vital piece of urban infrastructure. The design team aims to re-fit this industrial conveyance into a post-industrial instrument of leisure." What marks their design as unique among New York City's many recreational spaces is what they found: the 5.9-acre stretch of track, elevated 30 feet above ground, that meanders through 22 city blocks from 34th Street to Gansevoort Street, weaving in and out

1

of public and private spaces, through neighborhoods as diverse as the Chelsea art gallery quarter and the Meatpacking District.

The design relies on the raw structure of the High Line to give the project an urban character and counters this with a design marked by "openness" and "slowness," an escape from the chaotic streets below. Corner refers to the design as "perpetually unfinished," meaning that it will allow the spaces to evolve over time and leave them open for appropriation and new uses.

The system of planks that form the overall framework for their design are built from individual pre-cast units, and either fold down or are cantilevered up. They provide tapered pathways throughout the structure, preserving the unique form of the High Line and maintaining its existing variegated

landscape of woodlands, grasslands, and wetlands. The line is made accessible to all by planks that fold down to form ramps, and by stairs and elevator shafts cradled by the metal structure. The many gathering spaces, linear benches lining pathways, high chairs, and leaning bars provide places for groups to come together and take advantage of the views. These spaces, by encouraging lingering, allow for programmed and unscripted activity along the line.

One of the most interesting aspects of the High Line is its ability to form a new method of transportation throughout this section of Manhattan, linking neighborhoods that are both commercial and residential and providing a unique vantage point on the city. Vertical connections to the street grid below every three or four

blocks help ensure the line is accessible along its entirety.

In spring 2005, construction began on the first phase of the design from Gansevoort Street to 15th Street. This stretch will serve as a prototype for the remaining section of the line. As the project unfolds, the possibilities grow for the transformation of this industrial site into an unprecedented new space for activity and relaxation that works to forge links along Manhattan's burgeoning West Side.
—ZR

1 Aerial view of the High Line, New York, New York
2 Planking and planting concepts for High Line
3 Context plan for the High Line
4 Paving concept for the High Line

2

PIT
0% : 100%

PLAINS
40% : 60%

BRIDGE
50% : 50%

MOUND
55% : 45%

RAMP
60% : 40%

FLYOVER
100% : 10%

3

4

Oakland Waterfront Trail

Hood Design, EDAW, Murakami Nelson   Oakland, California   2007

The Oakland Waterfront Trail, a $53 million waterfront redevelopment project approved by the citizens of Oakland, California, in November 2002 is expected to be completed in 2008. The master plan called for a new 6.6-mile recreational trail along the industrial waterfront and was developed by a predominantly Oakland-based team led by EDAW with architects Murakami Nelson, landscape architects Hood Design, and geotechnical and environmental engineers Treadwell & Rollo. The trail will create a continuous connection between Jack London Square, one of Oakland's major intersections, and the international airport. It will provide connections to the waterfront for nearby residents and create new spaces for recreation, cultural events, and other activities intended to stimulate development and improvements for this part of the city.

Oakland's Estuary is already a popular site for boaters, joggers, bicyclists, and families. The trail will build on this engagement and provide a structured route along the water that connects neighborhoods, fosters community integration, and stimulates use of Oakland's existing waterfront nature reserves and parks. The existing pathways will be connected to a larger system of walkways and bicycle paths that could join up with roads leading inland at points, creating further visual and physical linkages between the city and the waterfront. A neighborhood workshop helped identify where new segments of the trail would be immediately achievable and which ones would need to be phased in at a later stage.

The trail will be 12 feet wide, widening to 15-20 feet where site conditions allow. At sections, individual parks, waterfront parks, and shoreline

access points will provide places of respite. These will be augmented with floating bridges, decks, and overlooks that extend beyond the shoreline to provide different experiences of the water and the natural environment.

Walter Hood, the California-based landscape architect who developed the major landscape elements for the trails, describes the project as reflecting the waterfront's historic and contemporary landuse. "Different areas have been created that 'mine' the physical, environmental, and social patterns and history." The resulting hybrid spaces can accommodate multiple uses to ensure that a range of activities occur along the water's edge. —ZR

1 Open space plan for Oakland Waterfront Trail, Oakland, California

2 Oakland Waterfront Trail shoreline map

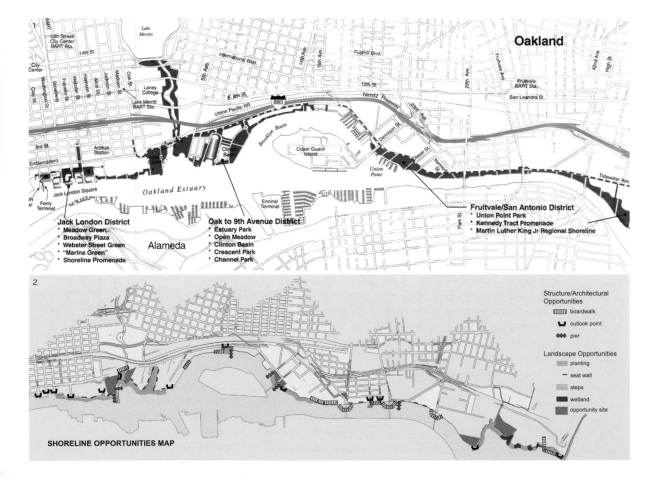

Jack London District
* Meadow Green
* Broadway Plaza
* Webster Street Green
* "Marina Green"
* Shoreline Promenade

Oak to 9th Avenue District
* Estuary Park
* Open Meadow
* Clinton Basin
* Crescent Park
* Channel Park

Fruitvale/San Antonio District
* Union Point Park
* Kennedy Tract Promenade
* Martin Luther King Jr Regional Shoreline

SHORELINE OPPORTUNITIES MAP

Structure/Architectural Opportunities
- boardwalk
- outlook point
- pier

Landscape Opportunities
- planting
- seat wall
- steps
- wetland
- opportunity site

Can You See Me Now?   Blast Theory and Mixed Reality Lab   Worldwide   2001-

Blast Theory develops interactive media works that include video and mixed-reality games which are played simultaneously online and in urban public spaces. In 2001, they were commissioned by the BBC and Arts Council England to develop *Can You See Me Now?* The game, first played in Sheffield in 2001, involves players chasing one another around a city with the aid of handheld Global Positioning System devices. Online players begin the game within a virtual map of the city. The runners on the ground are tracked by satellites and appear on the online players' maps. Using their handheld computers, the runners attempt to track down the online players (who are following the runners' movements virtually) while racing through the city. If a runner gets within 15 feet of an online player, they take a photo of the exact spot where they "saw" them, and the game is over. —ZR

1 Gamer playing in Rotterdam, the Netherlands

99 Red Balloons	Jenny Marketou and Katie Salen	San José, California	2006
Karaoke Ice	N. Nowacek, K. Salen, M. Zurkow	San José, California	2006

New media designers and artists Jenny Marketou, Katie Salen, Marina Zurkow, and Nancy Nowacek develop projects that employ technology and game design in public space. Their primary interest is in projects that develop social networks.

The most recent game, *99 Red Balloons*, incorporates interactivity and group actions. Based on an earlier game, *Flying Spy Potatoes*, nine players take on the roles of "Spy Fairies." Each fairy, armed with a large helium balloon and a wireless video camera, is assigned to a different area of the site, and has to navigate this territory with the help of passersby whom they persuade to play the game. As they play, they stream video recordings of the site to the game's headquarters. At the end of the 45-minute game, players return to the headquarters to choose a winner based on who they think navigated the space the best and engaged the public the most.

Karaoke Ice is a different type of project but involves similar ideas about community engagement. The design

team transformed an ice-cream truck into a mobile karaoke unit for public use. The project furthers their interest in social interactivity. Drawing on popular culture, they create works that are accessible and readily engage the public. —ZR

1 *Flying Spy Potatoes*,   2, 3 *Karaoke Ice*,
New York, New York   San José, California

Power Station London

ATOPIA, led by Jane Harrison and David Turnbull, is a design firm based in London, with a studio in New Jersey near Princeton University, where they teach. Their work fuses strategic planning, architectural design, product design, and environmental graphics. Their largest project to date is a new media and communications system for the redevelopment of Battersea Power Station in southwest London. Situated on 36 acres of open land on the south bank of the Thames, the former power station was designed in 1939 by architect and engineer Sir Giles Gilbert Scott, ceased operations in the early 1980s, was bought in 1993, and is now being converted into a 24-hour mixed-use commercial and entertainment complex, flanked by offices and housing. It is hoped that construction will begin in 2008 and that at least part of the redeveloped power station will be open in time for the 2012 Olympic Games in London.

The $2.8 billion project is being masterminded by Cecil Balmond, deputy chairman of Arup. Architect Sir Nicholas Grimshaw is in charge of remodelling the power station building itself into an arts and exhibition venue with a hotel on the rooftop to be designed by Ron Arad. Landscaping is being designed by Rotterdam-based West 8 and Gustafson Porter based in London and Seattle.

ATOPIA has been commissioned to tie the site's disparate parts together through a high-tech navigation, information, and communications system. Visitors will be able to access basic information including programs of events and exhibitions, schedules, directions, and listings for restaurants and bars. This information will either be available on screens, physically embedded on the site, or beamed electronically to handheld devices such as mobile phones and PDAs. Many of their initiatives require advanced communications infrastructure and the invention of new applications. The ultimate goal is to create a site-wide communications system that will be accessible to people on the site and on the internet. Harrison explains that "the project looks forward. It is designed for technology that will be readily available in five years, and provides an infrastructure that allows for that technology to be continually upgraded." ATOPIA is essentially redefining the standard information kiosk on an urban scale and creating what they refer to as a "managed environment."

ATOPIA is also designing architectural components, including the Platform, a public space in the central core of the Battersea Power Station. The building will function as an event space as well as be what ATOPIA calls this "Curator, DJ, and MC of the 'Power Station experience' for everybody individually and collectively, setting the scene and controlling the ambience." ATOPIA is also developing a series of gates and bridges throughout the power station complex to serve as communications hubs. For example, screens at the southeast corner entrance provide information, entertainment, and also an entry point to the site-wide wireless knowledge system. Harrison asserts "These meeting points provide places to plan your visit, learn where to go and how to get there, access special promotions and offers, and understand daily special events." —ZR

1 Battersea Power Station communications network, London, United Kingdom 2 Real and virtual connections 3 Battersea Power Station viewed from across the Thames

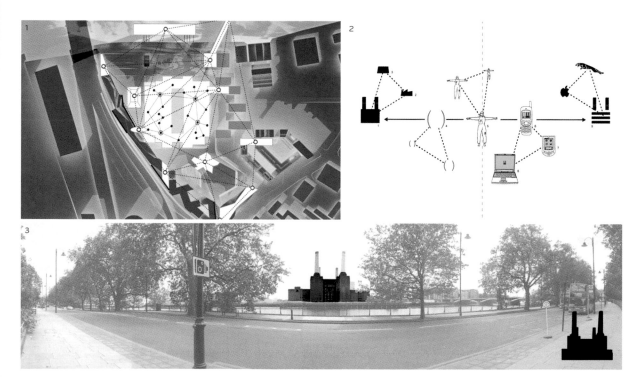

PITCH: Juba   ATOPIA research   Juba, Southern Sudan   2007

In addition to commercial projects, Jane Harrison and David Turnbull work on humanitarian initiatives as part of ATOPIA research, the non-profit arm of their practice that focuses on the relationship between informatics and ecology. In response to the radically changing political situation in Southern Sudan, ATOPIA is currently working to provide an immediate solution to the need for clean water. Juba is the largest and most developed city in Southern Sudan with a population of approximately 163,500. Devastated by civil war, the river port city is a collection of abandoned buildings, mud huts, and temporary compounds built by the international aid community. It lies at the southern terminus of traffic along the River Nile and is one of the largest concentrations of internally displaced people in the world.

ATOPIA research has developed a project in which soccer is understood as a catalyst that will invigorate communities and define a new kind of public space. The pitch simultaneously serves as a source of water, a place of assembly, an information hub to facilitate a collective awareness of a wide range of health issues (including the impact of HIV and AIDS), a site on which to grow the raw agricultural materials to support new cottage industries, and the space of athletic opportunity that can empower children and young adults. As Harrison puts it, "the water systems integrated into the pitch bring development goals, gender, and sport together and alleviate the extraordinary burdens placed on women who spend so much of their lives carrying water over long distances and are excluded from much of public life."

The design is decidedly low-tech. The pitch collects water in the gravel layers below the surface and filters it into the discarded shipping-container cisterns under the viewing terraces. The pitch delivers essential potable water to the larger community and uses the surplus to irrigate the circular field that surrounds it.

ATOPIA research will be developing the first cistern in 2007, and believes that others will follow, growing a network across the area and building consensus in an effort to bring people

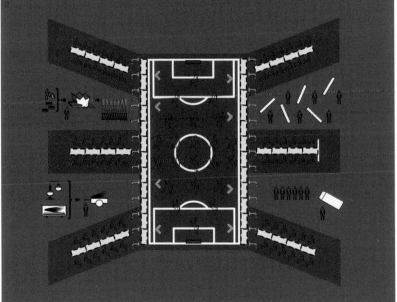

together and share local resources, ultimately leading to the construction of the pitch. As the designers have said, they "wanted to see if a soccer pitch and its surroundings could be made using reclaimed material, exploiting the surpluses that exist in even the most devastated situations." —ZR

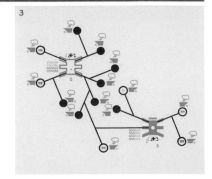

1 Soccer field and water collection concept, Juba, Southern Sudan 2 Plan of soccer pitch and water collection concept 3 Diagram for networking between water collection & soccer pitch

Pillow Fight Union Square	Newmindspace	New York, New York	2006
London Roof	Office of Subversive Architecture	London, United Kingdom	2002

Pillow Fight resembles a flashmob, in which a group of people assembles in a public space to perform an unexpected activity. Flashmobs and other types of organized swarming can be fun (mass bubble-blowing in Belgrade), absurd (a mob of naked bikers in Vancouver), activist (the Critical Mass movement), or subversive (Toronto's "hipster zombie" mobs). Newmindspace's *Pillow Fight*, however, is a combination between a public art project and an act of pure play. Organized via email, the event began when a few hundred people gathered in Union Square,

pillows in hand. As soon as the whistle blew, people began battling each other with the pillows—timidly at first, and then a bit more aggressively. Soon after, a few feather pillows tore open, and pretty much everyone was laughing.

In 2002, Office of Subversive Architecture invited 250 people to don translucent plastic suits and open black umbrellas, producing a mobile "roof" over London's Trafalgar Square. Funding the props themselves, and publicizing the event only via email, the project remained independent of commercial or political interests.

The group followed instructions to march and maneuver their umbrellas in unison, acting as a fluid, human "architecture" within the public square. While the scene recalls images of the military, industrial workers, or a crowd of mass consumers, the idea of *London Roof* seems at once to poke fun at our apparent blindness to the built environment, as well as to remind us of what really constitutes public space— people and their everyday movements and activities. —EY

1 *Pillow Fight Union Square*, New York, NY

2 *London Roof*, London, United Kingdom

Parkour

Parkour	David Belle	Worldwide	1985-

Parkour was invented by David Belle in 1985 in France. It involves traversing the city by running, jumping, and climbing over and under the obstacles of the built environment. The name derives from the French word *parcours* and practitioners are known as *traceurs*, referring to the act of tracing or drawing across the surface of the city. Belle writes that Parkour "is a natural method to train the human body to be able to move forward quickly, making use of the environment that's around us at any given time." —ZR

1, 2 Parkour *traceur* in London, United Kingdom

Yellow Arrow Projects

Counts Media Worldwide 2004–

Combining the high-tech playfulness of an urban game with the lo-fi intimacy of storytelling, the Yellow Arrow projects use mobile phone technology to publicize a personal narrative or forgotten story about a place. In the global Yellow Arrow project, yellowarrow.net users can obtain yellow arrow stickers to post anywhere in the world. Each sticker carries instructions for the person who finds it to send an SMS text-message to a New York phone number. Upon sending the message, they then receive a return text-message describing an anecdote or poetic observation about the site,

written by the person who first posted the sticker. —EY

1 *Yellow Arrow: The Secret New York*, Fulton Ferry Landing, New York, NY

2 *Yellow Arrow*, Lower East Side, New York, New York

Electronic Lens (e-Lens)

MIT Media Lab Manresa, Spain 2006

Countries around the world have been adopting mobile phones with Global Positioning System technology, offering location-based weather forecasts, tourist information, and news. The Electronic Lens project expands on this by providing users with access to civic and cultural information as they travel throughout the city. E-Lens was first tested in Manresa, Spain, as part of a government initiative to increase public participation in civil society. Students worked together to design architectural tours by first posting tags on buildings and then linking them to a database. Later, passersby could scan them using their specially programmed mobile

phones—or e-Lens—and instantly access this information. —EY

1 Students posting e-Lens tags in Manresa, Spain 2 Signs for e-Lens architectural tour

P2P: Power to the People

Gorbet Design Canada and USA 2002–

Originally designed for the 2002 Contemporary Art Forum, an annual art festival in Kitchener, Ontario, *P2P: Power to the People* reinterprets the old-fashioned electric advertising marquee, literally empowering participants with the ability to write a statement in lights, broadcasting their messages on a highly visible 30-foot sign. Inspired by a well-known slogan for the hydroelectric power industry, "Hydro for the People," *P2P* consists of an interactive billboard with 125 incandescent light bulbs, connected to a control panel with 125 corresponding light switches. While the project has

since been exhibited in several cities, the 2002 installation in Kitchener, in front of the City Hall, inspired perhaps the most interesting interactions between participants and the local authorities. Residents who typically did not have the opportunity to express themselves publicly, such as teenagers, punks, and homeless people, wrote profanities, inscribed political comments, and drew doodles on the billboard. —EY

1, 2 *P2P: Power to the People* installations in Kitchener and Toronto, Canada

Inbetween

erect architecture   London, United Kingdom   2005

In August 2005, Susanne Tutsch and Barbara Kaucky teamed up with local community organizations to hold the *Inbetween* treasure hunt as part of a plan to regenerate an area in Hackney, East London. The project was designed both as a tool for gathering input from residents on how to improve the neighborhood's open spaces, as well as a way to inspire residents to think differently about their relationship to the built environment. Following directions on a "treasure map," *Inbetween* encouraged participants to explore an area known for its diversity, but also for its abandoned and derelict public spaces. The map incorporates stories and games, and requests players to talk to as many people as possible. Erect architecture recently compiled a list of all the notes from the maps and used it as the basis for the design of a new community garden for the neighborhood. —EY

1 Detail of *Inbetween* map, London, UK

2, 3 Community garden, inspired by comments

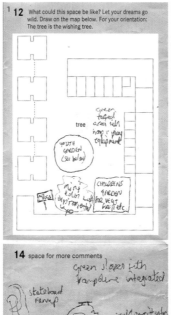

News.Box.Walk

Christina Ray (Glowlab)   New York, New York   2004

Brooklyn-based artist and curator Christina Ray creates interactive art projects inspired by Guy Debord's theory of the *dérive*, or the process of drifting through the city in response to objects and encounters, rather than having a planned destination. Many of these projects have been connected to her work with Glowlab, the artist collective and online publication which serves as a forum for developing ideas around urban public space. In August 2004, as part of the "1:100" exhibition, in which the interior of a Chelsea gallery was transformed into a 1:100-scale map of New York City, Ray created the *News.Box.Walk*, as "a guide to navigating the city by the patterns and locations of its brightly colored corner newsboxes." The walk begins on a corner where several newsboxes are located. Participants follow specific routes based on the colors and condition of the boxes. The game's objective is to provide a new perspective on the forces at play in public space. —EY

1, 2 *News.Box.Walk*, Union Square, New York, NY

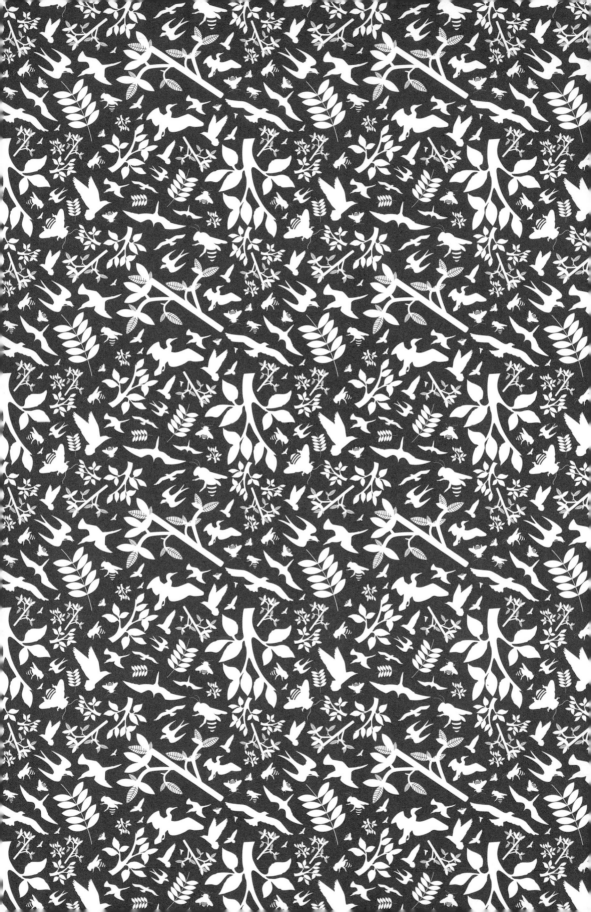

the healthy city

We all want to live in greener, healthier, and safer cities. The quality of the built environment is a barometer of a community and has a crucial impact on how cities operate, and in turn, on how we function and develop. Yet achieving healthy bodies, minds, and places is triggering unease in urban areas across the globe. Environmental and ecological concerns, increasing levels of poor health in underprivileged areas, and socially corrupt environments are just some of the warning signs that we need to clean up our acts, fast. Since Frederick Law Olmsted designed Central Park in 1858, investment in parks and open spaces has been shown to add value to urban regeneration schemes and provide health and educational benefits. Urban greenways and playgrounds curb levels of pollution, encourage physical activity, and promote social cohesion, helping to establish sustainable neighborhoods and communities.

The Healthy City projects illustrate how existing spaces are being rethought to accommodate new uses. The projects explored here help us to relax, exercise, socialize, develop skills, and facilitate learning—vital components of any thriving urban environment. Whether in Santa Fe, Buenos Aires, Malmö, Amsterdam, Seattle, or the German city of Eberswalde, spaces for play and cultural exchange are being reinvented on former industrial waterfronts, transportation interchanges, brownfield sites, vacant lots, and reclaimed land. Through extensive remediation and inventively adapting these under-utilized sites for new uses, architects and designers are triggering new developments and activities across the urban frame. In addition to creating new destinations, designers in Toronto and Manchester are generating concepts for innovative transportation routes for cyclists, pedestrians, and even swimmers. These forward-looking schemes propose environmentally conscious alternatives to traveling by car. Together, *The Healthy City* projects propose visionary ways of elevating the quality of urban public life with careful thought given to the well-being of the planet and its citizens. —ZR

roundtable discussion

diana balmori
principal, balmori associates landscape
architecture and VAI trustee

adrian benepe
commissioner, new york city department
of parks and recreation

andrew darrell
new york regional director,
environmental defense

ken smith
principal, ken smith landscape architect

cliff sperber
executive director, new york road
runners foundation

paul stoller
principal, atelier ten

andrew winters
director, office of capital project development,
office of the deputy mayor for economic
development and rebuilding

*The following conversation took place in
spring 2005 at Van Alen Institute. This text is
an edited version of the original transcript.*

balmori Frederick Law Olmsted's designs for parks
are currently being revisited as health-givers.
It is strange to see this health rubric, which was so
important to the 19th-century parks movement
and then forgotten, reappear. Although many of
the health concerns today are different, his idea
about creating the country in the city has come full
circle. Are new discussions forming around these
ideas or are they being adapted to current environmental ones?

sperber What interests me about Olmsted and
the parks movement in the 19th century is that
the parks weren't just for physical health but also
mental health.

darrell The parks movement also strived to provide
relief from what people believed to be unhealthy
urban environments—poor air quality, lack of
opportunities to experience the landscapes of
nature. The ideas were a remarkable combination
of how a natural environment—in the center of
a city—could foster health and social interaction
among people from different backgrounds and
social spheres.

sperber Olmsted wrote a great deal about the
impact of nature, particularly on the lower
classes—how they would benefit from coming
into contact with the upper classes. It would be
interesting to see what he would think of Central
Park today. He could not have anticipated that
hundreds of people would run around in spandex.
   Of course, what everybody understands now
is the connection between healthy air and healthy
people, hence the need for plants and trees. For
example, plants that produce oxygen and process
carbon dioxide help lower the asthma rates.
   It is the linear connector that is key to
Olmsted's idea. In Central Park, the East Drive
promenade runs the length of the park and
functions as social space that ties home, neighborhood, and work together. It is those linkages
that are really being lost in cities today.

smith The other link that we have lost in cities is
with agriculture and food production. Cities used to

be surrounded by agriculture and food production. Now people do not have a connection to where their food comes from. There are farmers markets such as the one in Union Square in New York City, which is very popular, but it strikes me that access to food production might be a new kind of recreation model.

benepe OK, we will turn the Great Lawn in Central Park into a tomato patch.

darrell When I was growing up, there was often a perception that being in the city was unhealthy. If you wanted to be healthy, you had to leave the city and visit nature. Nature was a place far away. Now, I see real changes in that perception fueled in part by better air quality, more access to parks, and an understanding of the health benefits of simply walking. There are so many new schemes for revitalizing the waterfront and tying together neighborhoods with green spaces along the water's edge. I feel like the idea of a healthy city is within reach.

I used to volunteer for a New York sailing club. We would take kids out sailing on the Long Island Sound. One Sunday, I was dropping a student off in West Harlem and I asked him if he enjoyed the weekend and he said, "Yeah, it was really great. I wish I lived near the water." And literally, you could see the Hudson River right outside the windshield of the van. So it was not that he did not live near the water but that he had no access to it. Now, that is beginning to change citywide, with projects like Harlem on the River, the Bronx River Greenway, East River Park, and Hudson River Park.

sperber The New York Road Runners Foundation serves thousands of children a week in public schools by providing running programs. One of our challenges is finding space in which the kids can run. Many of the school yards are littered with parked cars or debris. If you want to improve the health of the population, you have to help those most at risk. That is the hard part. In the same neighborhoods where obesity rates are highest, there is also the least leisure time, the most work time, the least safety, and the least opportunity

to get out in public space. I think one of the challenges is the question of organic recreation as opposed to hyper-planned recreation.

balmori That means more attention to streets— not just the parks.

winters The city's greenway system is a good example. It will connect neighborhoods and allow for access to open space throughout the city.

benepe Already we are seeing a difference with the greenways along the Hudson River. Talk about "build it and they will come." We created one bike path that runs the length of Manhattan along the West Side and already, it is overcrowded.

darrell I think even just striping a bikeway down on an existing city street is a huge step towards achieving a greenway. The visibility helps open people's perception to bikes as a viable choice. The incremental accessibility allows people who would not normally bike down a busy street to try it and to see others using the bike lanes safely. Bike lanes can connect parks and connect neighborhoods.

stoller I think that is really important. I think we have to stop seeing greenways as just things that are on the waterfront. They also function in the middle of cities and along major avenues.

benepe This is happening in Greenpoint and Williamsburg in Brooklyn. I have talked to Amanda Burden, chair of New York City Department of City Planning, about collaborations with New York City's Department of Transportation to work on spurring new kinds of developments such as these that do not take major initiatives, such as rezoning, to make them happen.

stoller I want to touch on how you pay for these changes. One of the things that I see from the Hudson River Park project is that if you put a nice park out on the waterfront it affects real estate value. Real estate brokers are marketing the park as part of their pitch for selling apartments in the West Village.

balmori Olmsted always put forward that argument as a way to convince people to build parks and as an argument for how to pay for them. In Minnesota, people pay a separate tax for parks and the money is used to maintain them.

benepe New York City's capital budget for parks is about $800 million, which is way beyond that of any other American city. It shows. Parks in New York have gotten a lot better in the last 20 years. We make it work through public-private partnerships.

balmori Do we still need the park conservancies?

benepe I think you need them to ensure the participation of people. I don't really favor policies that enable wealthy parks to get wealthier. Some of the money saved by the Central Park Conservancy has been used on projects in the Bronx and Brooklyn. People in Manhattan may resent that but it is actually better for everyone.

balmori American cities are always looking to attract private investment. Yet, we know from experience that there is a limit to the percentage of additional money that will be spent by a private developer on public space. The French government has agreed to spend $600 million in Paris for environmental purposes, mainly on public spaces, to mention another way of doing things.

darrell There are lots of ways to engage the private sector. Companies will respond to incentives. The public and the private play a symbiotic role.

balmori Another European example is Germany. The government is providing deductions in taxes to those who develop green roofs on their buildings.

smith When we think about parks, we also have to think about basic geography differences. I've been working on a park in New Mexico. They get 11 inches of rain a year, 13 in a good year. Our park will get no municipal water for irrigation. We are working with the Trust for Public Land, which is helping to raise the money for this park.

Because the park is part of the old railyard, we are in talks with the neighboring buildings to secure the rights to their roof water. A big part of the infrastructure of our park is a fairly sophisticated water collection storage system.

stoller One of my favorite parks is André Citroën Park in Paris. At the top of the park, there is this fantastic water fountain. There are signs along it that say, "Don't play in the water." But of course, it is full of kids playing in the water, and it is fabulous.

benepe In New York, there are about 600 spray showers for kids in the playgrounds. Having more opportunities for children to play with water and sand is very important. Tragically, for a while we were getting rid of sandboxes because they are hard to keep clean. But we are going to start integrating sandboxes again. We will figure out a way to keep them clean.

sperber I wonder whether our assumptions about parks and recreation are universal. The city's population looks really different now than it did 30 years ago. It is estimated that 400,000 Mexican families live here now, and 49% of the city is foreign-born. People come from countries where public space looks very different.

benepe We have to make changes. Queens is a good example in this regard. Flushing Meadows is an area with a large immigrant population. There was a big park with a lot of tennis courts that were not being used. Instead we simply laid out an artificial turf soccer field. It is completely full at the weekends. There were other issues that followed. Alongside the soccer fields, illegal vendors starting selling food. Instead of throwing them out, we legalized them. We created a co-op of vendors, got them Health Department permits and licenses for a small fee. These illegal vendors have become legal entrepreneurs.

smith I remember being struck in Paris by how much structured physical activity there was going on in community parks. They had giant 50-yard-long trampolines set up in particular areas and huge climbing frames for kids. Are we doing that kind of thing?

benepe Absolutely. We now have seven skate-board parks throughout the city. It was hard to figure out how to achieve these so that kids don't break their necks and sue us but we did it. There are dozens of swimming pools throughout the city. The newest thing that we're doing, particularly for inner city recreation, is turning asphalt play yards into synthetic turf sports fields. It used to be that if you were a kid in the inner city you would have lots of scabs all over your elbows and knees because you played on asphalt yards and fell. That is changing. In Harlem, for example, there are now six of these artificial turf fields. It means kids can play sports of any kind and not have to worry about falling and hurting themselves.

One of the biggest problems we face is creating the more adventurous kinds of facilities. Our state legislature is controlled by people who are part-time trial lawyers and who refuse to indemnify us from recreational activities. They force us to be nannies and build these really boring and safe places where there is no risk at all. We are slowly finding ways to make changes. For example, after many years of frustration, we have made it legal to surf at Far Rockaway Beach. We took the four-block area, where everybody has been surfing illegally for years and called it a surfing beach. We decriminalized surfing but we had to change the state health code to do it.

darrell I want to bring in another important issue—the question of design excellence and how we achieve this in cities.

benepe We have recently created the Design Excellence program particularly for this reason. This was an initiative spearheaded by Mayor Bloomberg. We now have a Deputy Commissioner for Capital Projects at the New York City Parks Department who is both a landscape architect and a historic preservationist. We have a chief of design. We take design seriously.

stoller What is important is to make sure is that the design process is considered part of the overall design of a place, which means that the appropriate questions are asked by the appropriate people to ensure the result is a success. Good design means more than getting good architects: it is about getting good project teams, for example, good engineers, good surveyors, and good water specialists. If ecological design is a goal for the design process, we must get people with particular expertise.

balmori Another important issue is the temporary use of public space and creating places that allow for unprogrammed, spontaneous, and temp-orary interventions. It is important to have a temporary category for the use of public space for spontaneous and temporary interventions.

winters One of my favorite things in the 19th century was the floating swimming pool that would be moored at the edge of the city on the river during the summer for public use. We have not had them in New York for a long time but I know the Neptune Foundation is trying to implement the idea again. Adrian, you have to do it!

Santa Fe Railyard Park

Ken Smith Landscape Architect, Mary Miss, and Frederic Schwartz Architects

Santa Fe, New Mexico

2007

In 2001, the City of Santa Fe and Trust for Public Land, a non-profit land conservation organization focused on preserving parks, gardens, and historic sites, organized a design competition for a new public park on the site of a former railyard in downtown Santa Fe. In May 2002, an eleven-member team headed by landscape architect Ken Smith, architect Frederic Schwartz, and artist Mary Miss was awarded the commission for the Railyard Park and Plaza.

The ten-acre park and two-acre plaza, which have a combined construction budget of $7.5 million, are part of a larger initiative to revitalize the city. The plan includes new commercial and residential buildings, a cineplex, restaurants, and bars. The new park and square are meant to create a central focus of public activity that will forge connections between the existing cultural institutions, including SITE Santa Fe, Warehouse 21, and El Museo Cultural. A new home will also be built for the Santa Fe Farmers Market on the main plaza.

"From the start, our main goal was finding ways to create a design that made visible the environmental aspects of the site," Smith notes. The former industrial site, that has a 400-year-old irrigation ditch running through it, is characterized by abandoned warehouses, seldom-used railroad tracks, and neglected open spaces. Most influential, however, is the area's dry climate. The region gets 11 inches of rain a year so the park has to have a self-sufficient water system. Rainwater will be collected in blue tanks and through an underground drainage system. Drought-resistant plants will be used so that the park will require little municipal water. A large tank at the center of the new public plaza combines the symbolic iconography of the railyard with the need to collect rainwater from the roofs of the surrounding buildings. The tank provides a shaded central seating area and has been designed to function as a drip fountain that funnels water back into the underground storage tanks.

In addition to the water storage issues, the design team was interested in emphasizing the history of the parkland as a former railyard. Looking

at old maps of the site, they uncovered the old rail lines, which presented an organizational system for the park's pathways and trails that cut across the park and connect to the city street grid. The design also incorporates a ramada, a traditional Spanish arbor that creates a much-needed shaded area and a social space.

Smith asserts that their design respects the goals of the brief, which was compiled following a master planning process and a series of community workshops in the late 1990s, executed by local firm Design Workshop. "In a pluralistic society, many people bring many interests to a public space. I am interested in creating spaces where this larger generosity is found," Smith explains. "Good design is making a park where different people can bring their own ideas and content to it." Mindful of the existing communities and the prospect of development, the park is designed to incorporate a number of flexible spaces that can be either programmed for community activities or left for appropriation by users. These include larger spaces for gatherings like the sloped performance terraces and open fields as well as more intimate spaces like small gardens and picnic groves for quieter activities and repose. The hope is that the park will become a focus for public life in the city and a place shared by the community. —ZR

1, 2 Detail of Santa Fe Railyard Park, Santa Fe, New Mexico 3 Plan of Santa Fe Railyard Park 4 Entrance to Santa Fe Railyard Park

3

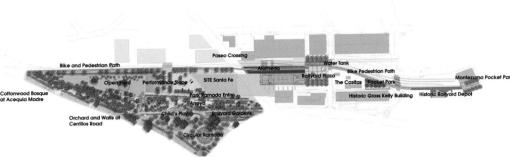

Bike and Pedestrian Path

Paseo Crossing

Water Tank

Alameda

Bike Pedestrian Path

Open Field

Railyard Plaza

The Casitas   Pocket Park

Montezuma Pocket Park

Cottonwood Bosque
at Acequia Madre

Performance Slope

SITE Santa Fe

Park Ramada Entry

Historic Gross Kelly Building

Historic Railyard Depot

Orchard and Walls at
Cerrillos Road

Arroyo

Child's Play

Railyard Gardens

Circular Ramada

River Coast Park

Arch. Claudio Vekstein   Buenos Aires, Argentina   2001

The Río de la Plata delta, which runs along the east edge of Buenos Aires, was once a popular stretch of urban beach. However, during Argentina's military dictatorship from 1976 to 1983, the river became a symbol of the country's political regime. Access to the water was closed to the public and private clubs emerged along the waterfront. During the 1990s, a city-led initiative to reclaim the water's edge for public use failed to obtain the land from the club owners. Faced with this challenge, the municipality of Vicente López, a city approximately ten miles north of Buenos Aires and part of the greater metropolitan area, decided to reclaim a landfill site in front of the clubs on which they could develop a new public park. In 1999, the city turned to local architect Claudio Vekstein to develop a design. Vekstein had already been working on the site to spearhead a campaign to rebuild a pavilion that had stood nearby, designed in 1966 by Amancio Williams in honor of his father, the composer Alberto Williams.

The initial brief for the 45-acre park was twofold: to create expansive open green spaces centered on an outdoor amphitheater capable of accommodating 30,000 people for large-scale events. Working to a budget of $1.65 million, Vekstein focused on creating major road access to the site and developing the program of the park. The modulated landscape is lined with a series of pedestrian paths that connect to public facilities and food and drink kiosks. The lowest levels of the site are periodically flooded and the highpoints of the park become green islands dotted with lighting, which Vekstein describes as a metaphor for the fireflies that are commonly seen there and "as an homage to the missing souls," the 30,000 people who disappeared during the military regime. The amphitheater sits at the highest point and has become a popular public gathering space, restoring the relationship between the city and its environment. —ZR

1 River Coast Park, Buenos Aires, Argentina
2 Amancio Williams Monument, River Coast Park 3 Lighting at River Coast Park
4, 5 Aerial views of River Coast Park

Post-Industrial Park

Topotek1   Eberswalde, Germany   2002

In 1998, the City of Eberswalde in northern Germany organized a competition for a new park on a former industrial site adjacent to the Finow Canal as the centerpiece of the Landesgartenschau 2002, a horticultural exhibition. The goal was to transform the site for public use, but rather than highlighting the characteristics of the former industrial site, the brief called for a park that accentuated topographical features and extant natural elements. The winning entry by Berlin-based landscape architects Topotek1 presents a bold graphic identity for the project that helps visitors navigate its vast terrain and differentiate its distinct sections. The design team, headed by principals Martin Rein-Cano and

Thilo Folkerts, explains that rather than "industrial romanticism" they took a pragmatic approach to the site, enhancing orientation and encouraging exploration and integration of people and activities.

The defining element of the design is a series of 15-inch-wide steel bands that traverse the entire site. The lines begin at the old rolling mill and could be mistaken for a relic of the former steel production plant. The bands mark the site and differentiate it from the adjacent urban setting and dense forest landscape beyond. From a platform 100 feet above the ground, at the top of the Montagne Eber, visitors can gain an overall sense of the park's structure. Inspired by museum displays and the formal presentation of exhibits, the

steel bands demarcate 26 individual gardens. A garden of scents illustrates the effect of various flowers and plants on the mind and the body. One garden, bifurcated by a wooden trellis, creates a shady corner and a place of repose, and another, dotted with fans, provides cool breezes. A garden near the water provides views of the canal boats. A promenade lined with plane trees acts as the park's spine, providing unobstructed views that aid orient-ation. Rather than taking a nostalgic approach to this brownfield site, Topotek1 has created a stylized design that emphasizes bright colors, legibility, and variability to create a contemporary landscape. —ZR

1, 2 Aerial view of   Eberswalde, Germany
Post-Industrial Park,   3, 4, 5 Detail views

Dania Park   Thorbjörn Andersson and PeGe Hillinge   Malmö, Sweden   2002

Dania Park in Malmö, Sweden, designed by Stockholm-based architects Thorbjörn Andersson and PeGe Hillinge of SWECO FFNS Architects, is the first park to be built in the city for 50 years. Built on a flat industrial landfill site on the edge of the Øresund Sound, it is part of the new Western Harbor development. Formerly the site of a Saab factory, the contaminated land is unsuitable for large areas of plantings and trees. Instead, the park is characterized by a range of architectural features such as terraces, raised platforms, balconies, and a great lawn, which encourage a variety of activities from sunbathing and strolling, to jogging, swimming, and even climbing. Visitors can gain access

to the sea via three ramped slipways that are separated by concrete walls on either side. A solid granite wall at the rear of the walkways is embedded with seating that creates resting places and lookout points along the coastline. The walls also shelter visitors from harsh winds. Where possible, a double row of trees and low, salt-resistant shrubs have been planted to provide additional protection in bad weather. During the summer, however, visitors gather and relax on exposed terraces that jut out from the land over the sea. A row of wooden balconies overlooks the focal point of the project, a 100,000-square-foot sunken grass meadow that can accommodate 10,000 people. At the edge of the lawn

is a 25-foot-high wooden bastion that frames the landscape. Although not sanctioned by the local authorities, young people delight in using the wall as a climbing frame. Different-sized spaces encourage a range of activities from informal to more programmed events. Whether intimate or large-scale gathering areas, they are all oriented towards the water and take advantage of their seaside location. By creating a park on this post-industrial wasteland, Malmö has created a new, open social space that contrasts sharply with the density of the adjacent city. —ZR

1 Dania Park, Malmö, Sweden

2 Bastion at Dania Park

3 Viewing platform

Park and Jog

Buschow Henley   Manchester, United Kingdom   1999

The *Park and Jog* concept was developed by Buschow Henley (BH), a London-based architectural practice whose work focuses on the social and psychological impact of the built environment. Inspired by "Park and Ride" schemes that encourage shoppers to park their cars outside of city centers and make the return trip using public transportation, BH's utopian scheme offers some healthier options. It takes as its point of departure the need for more sustainable methods of commuting that assist urban renewal processes by improving "the local environment, regenerating the surrounding building stock, and improving the health of commuters."

Their proposal was envisioned for a one-mile-long stretch of road west of Manchester's center. BH proposes reducing the lanes for traffic from six to two, designating one of these as a bus lane and appropriating the remaining three for commuters traveling by alternate methods. One lane is covered in grass, another with a channel of water and another with sand. Parking their cars at the multi-story car park, commuters can change in the facilities provided and continue east into the city by either walking, jogging, cycling, rollerblading, horse riding, swimming, or rowing. The park terminates at Salford Central Station where BH envisions a special Suit Park that will provide commuters with a place to "shower and change into their suits." Commuters can return to their cars either via the three-lane park or by train.

Although the concept was originally conceived for Manchester, the designers believe that it is flexible enough to be adapted for any urban setting. BH hopes that encouraging new transportation methods that combine the ideologies of the health club with commuting can not only encourage healthier lifestyles but can also activate the urban environment, forge links throughout metropolitan areas and their communities, and create new experiences to enhance the life of the city.
—ZR

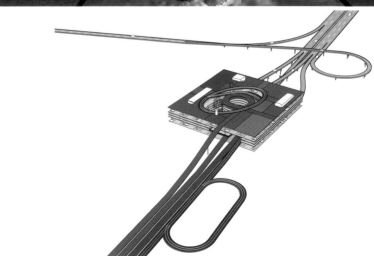

1, 2 *Park and Jog*   United Kingdom
concept, Manchester,   3 Car park and trails

Olympic Sculpture Park

Weiss/Manfredi   Seattle, Washington   2006

New York-based architects Weiss/Manfredi's design for a new Olympic Sculpture Park for the Seattle Art Museum is a bold response to the complex topography of the existing landscape. The eight-and-a-half-acre-site was purchased by the museum in 1999 with the aim of creating an outdoor exhibition space for its collection of modern and contemporary art. The site was formerly a fuel storage and transfer station and is characterized by a 40-foot drop to Elliot Bay. The budget for the park is $85 million, which includes extensive excavation and remediation, salmon habitat restoration, and sustainable design initiatives, including studies into native plants that reflect the local environment and will flourish in this exposed landscape. The site is divided into three parcels by a four-lane road and the tracks of the Burlington Northern Santa Fe Railroad, which are still in use. This complex set of conditions calls for a design that unifies the landscape and yet allows for a series of flexible exhibition areas.

Weiss/Manfredi's design solution involved bridging the space with a 2,200-foot-long zigzag path that reconnects the city with its waterfront and creates a ramped landscape for multiple activities and uses. The continuously sloping landform encourages users to traverse the entire site, starting at the pavilion at the top (a multi-use venue for art, performances, and educational programs, with a café and underground parking) and finishing at a series of new urban beaches along the waterfront. As visitors make their way down through the site they come across a variety of artworks, either displayed alone in the landscape like Alexander Calder's *Eagle*, a sculpture made in 1971, or incorporated into the infrastructure of the park, like *Seattle Cloud Cover*, a new work by Teresita Fernandez. Her series of vividly colored images of different sky conditions are applied over the glass panels of a 220-foot bridge, creating a saturated environment that heightens the experience of the natural surroundings.

Supporting the layers of crushed stones covering the zigzagging pathway is a system of mechanically stabilized earth clad with overlapping pre-cast concrete panels, reinforced by layers of high-density polyethylene geo-grid fabric. Michael Manfredi explains that they liked "the idea of a material as simple as earth being combined with very sophisticated materials and engineering sequences" to create a single defining element that is the backbone of the park. Smaller pathways meander through the landscape, allowing for exploration of the site, and taking advantage of the spectacular views across the water and back into the city.

An additional goal of the project was to integrate native plantings that will not only create different landscape conditions for exploration and education but will also help in the

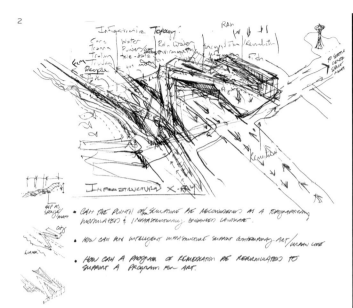

2

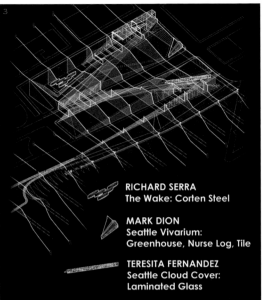

3

RICHARD SERRA
The Wake: Corten Steel

MARK DION
Seattle Vivarium:
Greenhouse, Nurse Log, Tile

TERESITA FERNANDEZ
Seattle Cloud Cover:
Laminated Glass

6

restoration of the land, through, for example, retention of rainfall above the soil surface. Three distinct landscape conditions inspired by the natural environment of the Pacific Northwest were developed with landscape architect Charles Anderson. At the top of the site near the pavilion is a dense forest including red cedar, sword fern, and vine maple trees. Further down is a deciduous forest of aspen trees and meadows of grass and wildflowers. Along the shoreline, new beaches protected by shrubs and grasses replace a seawall and will aid in the restoration of the coastline's marine ecology.

The park, which is free to the public and open year-round, is more than a sculpture park. It is a novel recreational space with jogging, bicycle and pedestrian paths, and a range of places in which to relax, gather, and play while enhancing the natural environment of the city. —ZR

1 Olympic Sculpture Park, Seattle, Washington
2 Diagram sketch
3 Topographic plan
situating artwork
4 Beachfront
5 Artwork in Olympic Sculpture Park
6 Olympic Sculpture

Northern Park

West 8

Amsterdam, the Netherlands   2010

In northern Amsterdam, approximately one mile from the center of the city, on the banks of the Noordhollandsch Canal, an underutilized park is about to be transformed by West 8, one of the Netherlands' leading landscape architecture firms. The 74-acre park that was once a peninsula at the top of the city was turned into a park in the early 1900s but has since fallen into ruin. The $37 million project is being funded by the municipality of Amsterdam as part of a redevelopment scheme for the northern area of

Amsterdam. The existing park reflects the typical landscape of northern Holland with flat planes divided by a central stretch of water lined with dikes. West 8's design redefines the park and provides a new identity for the area by inserting programmed spaces for active and passive recreation to be accessed via a greenway, which passes through a variety of different landscape conditions—from grass lawns to wooded areas to dense beds of plantings. West 8 compares the new design to New York's Central Park and

refers to some of its key elements in their design. For example, a road for joggers, cyclists, and rollerbladers loops around the park and is punctuated at points by access ways that link to the surrounding urban environment. Furthermore, Northern Park has been designed with a main bike lane that runs through the park, along the Noordhollandsch Canal. The road connects at two points to bridges that cross the canal, tying the distinct areas of the landscape together and creating a continuous route through the park.

It also links with the city's subway system at the entrance to the park, further enhancing connectivity between the park and neighboring communities. A border of ivy lines the pathway, which West 8 asserts creates "a mysterious, shadowy, yet transparent environment."

The Noordhollandsch Canal is the dominant element in the park. A series of dikes and a curved turning circle for boats give the park a distinct character. The linear position of the canal, running through the center of the landscape, provides opportunities for water-based activities throughout the park as well as scenic areas along the way for resting and lounging. The plan for the park incorporates three large open spaces which are situated parallel to each other. In the west there is an English garden with a gently sloping picnic lawn. Next to this is a slightly lower lawn with cafés and terraces, where small-scale events can take place. Adjacent to this is a deck raised over the water on pilings for activities such as skating. West 8 is known for its innovative urban design and landscape architecture projects and its in-depth working methods that strive to create context-specific solutions. For Northern Park, West 8 has created a design that does more than simply clean up the site. The new park rivals other urban parks in Amsterdam in size, waterfront location, and flexibility. —ZR

1 Aerial view of Northern Park, Amsterdam, the Netherlands

2 Plan of Northern Park

3, 4, 5, 6, 7, 8 Views of Northern Park

Velo-City

Chris Hardwicke   Toronto, Canada   2004

"It's Monday morning. You get your gear on and strap your bag onto your bike. It is cold and raining today but after five minutes riding you can see a glazed on-ramp in the distance. A quick lane-change and you pump your way up the ramp. Switching into the slow lane, you can already feel the draft pulling you forward as cyclists in the fast lanes blur past you and into the distance. Once you get your rhythm, your shoulders relax as you let down your defenses. No more cars breathing down your neck."

This is how architect Chris Hardwicke envisions a cyclist riding through *Velo-City*, a concept proposal for an elevated highway for bikes that connects through metropolitan areas. Mindful of the inadequate exercise endemic to our urban environments and the increasingly longer commutes people are forced to make as they relocate to the edges of the city, Hardwicke conceived of *Velo-City* for his hometown of Toronto, Canada. Toronto has one of the largest populations of cyclists in North America yet Hardwicke argues that the city has provided minimal infrastructure or support. In addition to the health benefits of more active lifestyles, Hardwicke argues that by promoting cycling, cities can reduce vehicular traffic and in turn air pollution—to say nothing of the need for bigger multi-story parking garages.

Velo-City is made up of two elevated highways. Traffic flows in opposite directions in each and there are three lanes for slow, medium, and fast travel. The structure, not dissimilar to an elevated roadway, is enclosed in glass to reduce air resistance thereby increasing the efficiency of cycling by about 90% and allowing for speeds up to 30 miles per hour. Hardwicke challenges cities to invest in *Velo-City* by locating it in existing spaces such as highways, power and railway corridors, or built into or through buildings and streetscapes. Hardwicke notes that transportation systems often define a place. His goal is for Toronto to one day be known for *Velo-City*. —ZR

1, 2 Interior views of *Velo-City*, Toronto, Canada   3 Exterior view   4 *Velo-City* bike station

thirteen tactics for the good life

iain borden

Central to *The Good Life* project is the proposition that architecture and design are not just about isolated buildings or eminent architects but are also about urban space and agents of all kinds being intimately connected with the fabric and machinations of city life. The joys of the city are then not confined to the interiors of buildings, or just to the way that they have been conceived, but rather are an expanded field which incorporates the full range of possible architectures—that, is, all kinds of objects, insertions, spaces, practices, ideas, and emotions.

To understand this view of architecture and urban life we must, therefore, consider the radical proposition that the relation between design and our experiences of cities is not singular, predictable, or even readily understandable, but is instead complex, unpredictable, and constantly changeable. This is not an easy condition to accept, but accept it we must.

So how to try and comprehend this notion of urban space and city life as inherently unstable and dynamic? Particularly relevant here are the thoughts of the French philosopher Henri Lefebvre on the social production of space, the everyday, and the politics of the city. In his numerous writings, Lefebvre, in short, proposes that social space is a social product, made by us through our own practices, codes, and experiences. Urban space, therefore, is not just about the great monuments of the city, but the places where we go about our everyday lives—where we work and commute, where we find passion and intimacy, and where we find smaller, body-scale spaces. Politically, the underlying contention here is of the right to the city as being something which should be open to all peoples, of whatever age, gender, class, ethnicity, or sexuality. Indeed, one of the central aims of urban life should be to not only tolerate but celebrate and encourage differences, creating a multitude of experiences, qualities, and spaces.

This kind of urban space is, then, diametrically opposite to the space of professionals, drawings, geometry, static objects, and strict urban managers. It is a space of fluid dynamics, subject to constant change not just in its forms and uses but in the very understandings that people—all of us, not just urban and design professionals—have of cities. Space, that is, which is provisional and significant, inclusive and yet varied, political and familiar, intense and subtle, exciting and calming, beautiful and stimulating. This is what Lefebvre called "differential space," a celebration of the sameness and difference between us all, a machine of possibilities where all urban citizens are free to express and develop themselves to the utmost of their potentials, desires, and abilities.

How then might this kind of space by constructed? This is where *The Good Life* steps right in, suggesting a myriad of designs, spaces, events, ideas, and experiences whereby city residents can help to create truly dynamic, healthy, and enjoyable worlds. What I wish to do here is to extrapolate—partly from Lefebvre and other urban theorists, partly from the *Good Life* projects, and partly from other similar projects worldwide—and in doing so propose a series of thirteen tactics which might be reused by designers, thinkers, and urban residents of all manner of cities.

01 Temporalities
Ever since the 19th century when the demands of the railway system and industrialized production led to the imposition of standardized time and regional time zones, capitalism and the modern city have increasingly marshaled us into various forms of schedule, appointments, meeting slots, diaries, calendar dates, and windows of opportunity. This is a regime of linear and artificial time, regulated by computers, management systems, and social conventions. Yet other times are also possible—times of the body and nature, times of moments, circularity, indeterminate length, and movement. And nowhere are such times more evident than in our parks and open spaces, which allow for romance, hand-holding, and even more overt displays of sexuality, which foreground the seasonal cycles of nature and weather, which allow for people to make up their own durations, from the momentary to lengthy. Public spaces insert different temporal rhythms into the city; as a bank of different kinds of temporality, parks are one of our most precious resources.

02 Performance
Cultural expression and, in particular, the related act of criticism are often confined to the codified realms of texts, buildings, and physical artworks—those productions which speak of authority and which imply a sense of stature and permanence. Yet, as theater, dance, poetry, and music all tell us, there are other ways of being critical, of saying things without writing things down, or of making objects in space. The good life of the city should incorporate all manner of spaces where people can gyrate, glide, and rotate, mime, perform, and declaim, climb, descend, and traverse, and act out opinions. Street poets, graffiti artists, and skateboarders already know this much, and their actions should be encouraged and celebrated—for it is here that cultural acts can be performed, witnessed, and heard.

03 Media
City spaces are often thought of too simply, as being just parks and plazas. But what are parks and plazas if not meeting places, or rather *potential* meeting places, where glances, touches, smiles, words, gossip, observations, and opinions of all kinds have the possibility of being transferred? City squares are information and relationship exchanges, allowing data and people alike to shuttle around in restless patterns of movement and co-presence. This condition can be intensified further by bringing non-physical spaces into our cities,

through screens, wireless networks, display boards, downloads and uploads, text messaging, podcasts, and broadcasts of all kinds. In this way, cities become at once real and virtual, physical and ethereal, concrete and imagined—truly composed of media of all kinds, and accessible at all times. The city is consequently transformed from a dead archive—where information is deposited and forgotten—into a living flux of information and communication.

04 Remembering

Choosing who and what to remember in cities is an important historical, political, and cultural decision. At times we choose to remember those great events and figures who help to define our nations and most commonly held beliefs. And at other times we choose to remember those figures and events which are embedded in our everyday lives but which still, thus, help us to find, as Georg Simmel called it in *The Philosophy of Money* (London: Routledge, 1990), "in each of life's details the totality of its meaning." Hence the need for memorials, statues, plaques, and festivals, and also minutes of silence, badges, markings, and artworks of all kinds of formats, scales, and technologies, all of which help to recall that which is at once ordinary yet extraordinary. In doing so, we create a different kind of monumental city and a differing kind of remembering—a testa-ment to the struggles, remarkable spirit, and lasting achievements of everyday urban citizens.

05 Quietude

So much of architecture and urban design is directed at the monument and the landmark—iconic objects which can be seen from afar, lending instant recognition to a whole city. Yet much of urban life is focused on more quiet aspects of the city, projects which speak gently and converse with us as friends might do during a Sunday promenade. I am thinking here of benches, ledges, walkways, simple squares, and meeting places—all of the most incidental of architectures—yet also of shops, libraries, and cafés, and even of museums, galleries, and theatres that do not seek to proclaim their presences with an immediate and unavoidable declamation. Compared to the architecture of shouting, these other, more retiring designs are like asides, off-stage whispers which create a complex atmosphere on the urban stage and a rich texture of architectural fabric.

06 Uncertainty and Risk

There are some things we need to know: the state of our water supply, traffic flows, demand for housing, energy supplies, and likely climate change. But there are other things which we need not to know, things which should remain uncertain, unclear, and unknown. Our city spaces therefore need to be dual in character, spaces in which we encounter otherness and sameness, where we are at once confirmed and challenged—and this comes from not being certain, from not knowing everything around us, from a degree of surprise and the unusual as we go about our everyday lives. We need a city which we do not know, which we do not understand, which we have not yet encountered, which is simultaneously strange, familiar, and unknown to us. This is public space which is always a surprise, a unique place of stimulation. This is the acceptable and indeed desirable risk of not always knowing what lies around the corner.

07 Provisional Identities

How do we define ourselves? Am I black, white, or any other color? Are you gay, straight, or bisexual? Is he a football, hockey, or opera fan? Are we Italian, Bolivian, American, Korean, or Kenyan? Is she a feminist or a socialist? Are they Conservatives, Democrats, or Greens? Do not seek to answer these questions with any certainty or confidence, for no longer do many members of the global community seek to proclaim permanent memberships of any single determining form of identity. No longer do we have a single identity which lasts relatively unchanged throughout our lives, but rather we have— or can have if we so choose to recognize the opportunity—multiple identities, fractured identities, and provisional identities which shift and mutate according to our age, body, city of residence, cultural tastes, and general attitude. In short, just as our lives shift in pattern and composition from year to year, week to week, even hour to hour, so too does our sense of who we are, who we might be, and who we desire to be. This is the way people are constantly being reconstructed and reimagined in cities today, and this is the way that cities must then be designed—not for predictable, monolithic sectors of the population (for these sectors are often but mirages, projections of the viewer rather than a true representation of the city), but for various different and competing tastes, opinions, and outlooks. The identities of our city spaces, like those of its inhabitants, should be multiple, diverse, and dynamic; energetic, ephemeral, and hybrid.

08 Fluidity

Boundaries mark social categories in space, inscribing the edges of territory, possession, authority, association, and even opinion Although undoubtedly necessary to demarcate our private homes and places of work, such boundaries do not always have to be frontal and brutal in their expression, not always challenging and confrontational to those who negotiate them. Boundaries can be thick, complex, gentle, staged, gradual, and even invisible, using stenography, texture, materials, technologies, and all manner of modulation in order to suggest to city dwellers whether they should, or should not, traverse the boundary in question. In this way, we ourselves are asked to regulate our behaviors in a subtle and responsible manner—which is much better than being immediately faced with an intimidating gate, guard, or sign. Fluidity, not obstacles, is the key.

09 Interventions

Architecture, by its very nature, tends towards colonization and domination—that is, it takes over a particular space, imposing by its materiality and arrangement of space a certain social order that prevents other activities from taking place. And of course we need such domination; we need the security of hospitals, homes, and schools, of offices, factories, and airports. And at other times we need different kinds of architecture, those which appropriate rather than dominate, and those which intervene and attach rather than impose and replace. We need architectures of an impermanent and temporary nature, which appear for a few weeks, days, or even hours, which do whatever it is that they need to do, and then disappear without leaving a trace (except, that is, in the minds of all those who witnessed it). Architecture in this way is like a seasonal flower: beautiful in its very ephemeral and provisional presence, and appreciated not only for what it provides, but also in the knowledge that it will, very soon, be gone.

10 Play

Play is no laughing matter. Seemingly silly and superficial, play undoubtedly invokes the childish delights of being mischievous and of testing the boundaries of acceptability. Yet underlying its surface veneer of infantilism, play is much, much more than that: it tells us that aggression in cities is latent and not always detrimental, that being ridiculous is okay, that all of us are in some way children at heart, and, above all, that our urban spaces are not just for the purposes of work, tourism, retail, and all that supposedly important stuff, but also for having fun, for letting go, for being ourselves in our full range of emotions and bodily extensions. Play is *serious* fun, and we should all be able take part.

11 Active Health

If play is what we should do, then how can we make it occur? Here we have much to learn from children, who often see no separation between their worlds of imagination and fantasy and their worlds of routine and chores. Rather, play exists everywhere, at home, in the schoolyard, in the back of the car, and at all times of the day. This provides clues as to how adults might stay healthy in cities, where too often healthy activity is solely confined to the self-conscious gym or regimented sports field. Active health means being energetic in all parts of our lives: bicycling rather than driving, walking up and down stairs rather than using the elevator, strolling rather than standing, standing rather than sitting...In this way health becomes part of the incidental elements of city spaces, such as walkways, stairs, bicycle routes, skating and running paths, all of those spaces where the body can be allowed to work just a tiny bit harder. Healthy activity is here fully embedded within the good life of the city, not zoned out into isolated spaces and times.

12 Active Thinking

Healthy citizens have healthy minds as well as healthy bodies, and the good life needs to be promoted in our thoughts as well as in our muscles. Hence the benefits of having architecture which provokes questions, which ask us to contemplate the world around us in a provocative and interactive manner. This is the very opposite of the shopping mall—where too often the only question we are asked is as to which commodity we should buy next—and is now a place where we are asked about politics, ethics, and morality, about the environment, nature, and climate, about friend, families, and desires ...not in a heavy-handed or challenging way, but in the same way in which such questions arise in music, films, artworks, and cultural products of all kinds. Our architecture, like all of our arts, should be a catalyst to thought, a prompt to puzzle over our cultures and cities.

13 Emotions

Nor do such thoughts always have to be logical, rational, or considered. Our emotions too should be nurtured and cultivated. Hence the need for city spaces which make us glad and sad, happy and doleful, excited and calm, delighted and disgusted, pleased and angry, sympathetic and dismissive, intrigued and repelled, energized, and relaxed. It is after all, the quality of emotional life which, for many city dwellers, lies at the heart of their urban existence. Without a full range of emotions—that is, without a full range of the meanings and possibilities of how it feels to be human—we are as yet unfulfilled, and the good life is yet to be achieved.

Iain Borden is Head of the Bartlett School of Architecture, University College London, where he is Professor of Architecture and Urban Culture. His recent publications include Manual: the Architecture and Office of Allford Hall Monaghan Morris *(2003),* Skateboarding, Space and the City *(2001),* The Unknown City *(2001), and* InterSections *(2000).*

project credits

Idea Store Whitechapel
London, United Kingdom, 2005
client London Borough of Tower
Hamlets architect Adjaye/Associates
design team David Adjaye (Principal),
Samson Adjei, Christopher Adjei,
Yohannes Bereket, Nikolai Delvendahl,
Jessica Grainger, Martin Kaefer, Haremi
Kudo, Sean McMahon, Yuko Minamide,
John Moran engineer Arup graphic
design Mode consultants Miller Mitchell
Burley Lane (Project Manager)
Arup Façade (Façade Consultant)

Denia Mountain Project
Denia, Spain, 2010
client City of Denia, Alicante,
Spain architect Guallart Architects
design team Vicente Guallart
(Principal), Max Sanjulian, Jordi
Mansilla engineer Robert Brufau
consultant Jose Miguel Iribas
(Sociologist)

SOMOHO
(Soweto Mountain of Hope)
Soweto, South Africa, 2002
client The Community of Tshiawelo,
Soweto initiator and architect
Mandla Mentoor and Katy
Marks design team Mandla Mentoor
(Initiator, Community Leader),
Katy Marks (Architect, Facilitator),
Mpumelo Sidyiyo, Jabulani
Banda, Tholakele Mentoor, Hilda
Nekhumbe, The Tshiawelo community
consultants Jon Nutt (Engineer),
Morag Campbell and Henry
Payne (Architectural Advisors),
John Clarke, Dr. Colin Hudson,
Christian de Sousa, Peter Khomane,
Jonathan Robinson, Roots and Shoots,
Refiloe Serota, Gaia Foundation

Stadium Culture
Novi Sad, Serbia, 2007
client Kuda.org—New Media Centre,
Novi Sad architect Srdjan Jovanovic
Weiss, NAO design team Srdjan
Jovanovic Weiss (Principal), Ivana
Sovilj, Thomas Julliard Zoli, Emir
Hadziahmetovic, Andreja Miric (Intern),
Dejan Mrdja (Intern), Dubravka Sekulic
(Intern) consultants Katherine Carl
and Zoran Pantelic (Programming),
Anna Dyson & Materialab (Solar
Façade Design & Research), Jane
Wernick (Structural Engineering),
d.i.a. Ruzica Jovanovic reg. urb.
(Urbanism & Research), d.i.a. Darko
Polic (Urbanism)

Eib's Pond Park
Outdoor Classroom
Staten Island, New York, 2000
client The Parks Council,
Green Neighborhoods Program
architect Marpillero Pollak Architects
design team Sandro Marpillero
(Principal), Linda Pollak (Principal),
Paul Teng, Gwynne Keathley,
Brett Thevenote partners Fox Hills
Tenant Association, Staten Island
(Reverend Hattie Smith-Davis,
President); Southern Queens Park
Association, Jamaica, Queens; NYC
Department of Parks and Recreation
construction Americorps Program
led by Kate Chura with Albin Thomas

Biblioteca degli Alberi
Milan, Italy, 2009
client City of Milan, Italy
project manager Inside Outside Team
design team Petra Blaisse (Interior/
Landscape Architect), Michael
Maltzan Architecture, Mirko Zardini
(City Planner/Theorist), Irma Boom
(Graphic Designer), Piet Oudolf
(Planting Design) engineer RoD'or:
Rob Kuster (Landscape Engineering)

Heerlijkheid Hoogvliet
Hoogvliet, the Netherlands, 2007
client Wimby!/Vestia
architect FAT design team Sam Jacob
(Principal), Sean Griffiths (Principal),
Charles Holland (Principal),
Matt Stack, Lizzie Evans associate
architect Korteknie Stuhlmacher
Architecten consultant Peutz (Acoustic
Consultants) engineers Pieters
Bouwtechniek (Structural Engineers),
Boersema Installatie Adviseurs
(M&E Engineers)

Homerton Struggle Niche
London, United Kingdom, 2005
client City Projects artist Nils Norman

Alexanderplatz
Berlin, Germany, 2005
artist RACA design team Johan
Carlsson (Principal), Pulsk Ravn
(Principal)

PARK(ing)
San Francisco, California, 2005
artist Rebar design team John
Bela (Principal), Matt Passmore
(Principal), Blaine Merker, Gregory
Kellett, Brady Moss

Guerilla Gardeners
Toronto, Canada, 2003-
organization Toronto Public Space
Committee design team Erin
Wood (Main Contact/Downtown
Coordinator), Lindsay Kelly (Annex
Coordinator), Heather MacDonald
(East End Coordinator), Andy Brown
(West End Coordinator), Tanya Hagen
(Research Coordinator)

GuerrillaGardening.org
London, United Kingdom, 2004-
client The Public
organizer Richard Reynolds

Coventry Phoenix Initiative
Coventry, United Kingdom, 2004
client City of Coventry master planner
and architect MacCormac Jamieson
Prichard design team MacCormac
Jamieson Prichard (Master Planners
and Architects), Modus Operandi
(Art Consultant), Rummey Design
Associates (Landscape Architects
and Urban Designers), Speirs
and Major (Lighting Designers),
Ashgate Development Management
Services (Project Manager), W T
Partnership (Cost Consultants)
engineer The Babtie Group (Transport
and Civil Engineers)

Public Art Projects
United Kingdom, Ireland, France,
Germany, 1996–2005

Railings
London, Paris, Berlin, 1996-
artist Greyworld

Bridge 2
Dublin, Ireland, 2000
client Guinness artist Greyworld

Bins and Benches
Cambridge, United Kingdom, 2005
client The Junction Theatre
artist Greyworld

Solkan Fountain
Solkan, Slovenia, 2001
client Local community of Solkan
architect Sadar Vuga Arhitekti

design team Jurij Sadar (Principal), Bostjan Vuga (Principal), Toncek Zizek, Milan Tomac, Marjan Poboljsaj, Mirjam Milic engineers Vojko Kilar (Structural Engineer), Primoz Banovec (Hydrodynamic Model Engineer), Peter Grabnar (Computer 3D Model Engineer), Marmor Hotavlje (Fountain Technology Engineer), Kono (Traffic/ Site Engineer)

Park Bench House
Melbourne, Australia, 2002
architect Sean Godsell Architects
design team Sean Godsell (Principal)

Römerkastell and Marktplatz
Stuttgart, Germany, 2003
client Wolfgang Kreis
architect and designer Dietrich Brennenstuhl and Nimbus Design

Public Art Projects
Siena and Udine, Italy, 2001, 2005

Play or Rewind
Siena, Italy, 2001
client Arsnova, Accademia di Arti Multimediali artist Cliostraat design team Matteo Pastore, Luca Poncellini, Alessandra Raso, Stefano Testa, Timothy Heys-Cerchio, Tim Power

Slacklines
Udine, Italy, 2005
client Villa Manin, Centro d'Arte Contemporanea artist Cliostraat design team Luca Poncellini, Alessandra Raso, Stefano Testa

Jumping Field
Helsinki, Finland, 2000
client Kiasma Museum of Contemporary Art, Helsinki artist Tommi Grönlund/Petteri Nisunen design team Tommi Grönlund, Petteri Nisunen consultants Pekka Matomäki, Matti Ollila Consulting Engineers Ltd

Contemporary Music Center
Taichung, Taiwan, 2008
client The City Government of Taichung architect Stan Allen Architects design team Stan Allen (Principal), Carlos Arnaiz (Project Architect), Nahyun Hwang (Design Collaborator), Kate Goggin (Design Collaborator) animation David Huang associate architect CitiCrafts, C. David Tseng

consultants Team 10 (Consultants for Performances, Arts and Technology), Eric Chaung, Lin Ke-Hua

Flux Park, King's Cross
London, United Kingdom, 2012
client Argent (King's Cross) plc.
group General Public Agency
design team Clare Cumberlidge, Lucy Musgrave, Justin Graham, Emily Greeves, Rebecca Bennett, Christian Sievers, Marianne Christiansen, Antonio Lipthay collaborators Public Works (Art & Architecture Collective): Kathrin Boehm, Sandra Denicke-Polcher, Torange Khonsari, Andreas Lang; Hyperkit (Digital designers): Tim Balaam, Kate Sclater; Townshend Landscape Architects (Landscape Architects); David Morley Architects (Architects); Helena Ben Zenou (Artist); Lottie Childs (Artist); Sophia Clist (Set Designer); Tim Gill (Play Expert); Pippa Gueterbock (Architect, Fluid); Seth Reynolds (Play Worker); Tricia Stainton (Horticulturalist)

North Plaza, Lincoln Center for the Performing Arts
New York, New York, 2009
client Lincoln Center for the Performing Arts, Inc. architect Diller Scofidio + Renfro design team Elizabeth Diller (Principal), Ricardo Scofidio (Principal), Charles Renfro (Principal), Gerard Sullivan (Project Leader), Ben Gilmartin (Project Leader), Josh Uhl, Robert Donnelly, Ben Mickus, Frank Gesualdi, Eric Howeler, Stefan Gruber, Michael Hundsnurscher, Rainer Hehl, Gaspar Libedinsky, Gerri Davis, Florencia Vetcher, Filip Tejchman associate architect FXFOWLE Architects structural + MEP engineering Arup, NY: Markus Schulte, Mahadev Raman

Barking Town Square
London, United Kingdom, 2007
client Redrow Regeneration, London Borough of Barking and Dagenham architect muf architecture/art design team Katherine Clarke (Principal), Liza Fior (Principal), Mark Lemanski, Alison Crawshaw

Grand Canal Square
Dublin, Ireland, 2008
client Dublin Docklands Development

Authority architect Martha Schwartz (In Association with Tiros Resources) design team Shauna Gillies-Smith (Principal in Charge of Design), Martha Schwartz (Principal), Friederike Huth (Project Manager), John Pegg, Paula Craft, Jay Rohrer, Jessica Canfield, Christian Weier associate landscape architect Tiros resources: Chris Kennett, Lucy Carey, Fran Vernon engineers Nicholas O Dwyer Limited, Omar Consulting Engineers lighting designer Speirs and Major Associates pavilion designer Grant Studio Architects

East River Waterfront Study
New York, New York, 2009
client The City of New York architect SHoP Architects and Richard Rogers Partnership design team SHoP Architects: Kimberly Holden (Principal), Gregg Pasquarelli (Principal), Chris Sharples (Principal), Corie Sharples (Principal), William Sharples (Principal), Catherine Jones, Matthew Liparulo, Steve Sanderson, Takeshi Tornier, Stephen Van Dyck; Richard Rogers Partnership: Richard Rogers (Principal), Michael Davies, Dennis Austin, Andrew Tyley landscape architect Ken Smith Landscape Architect: Ken Smith (Principal), Elizabeth Asawa, Alex Felson, Thomas Oles, Yuka Yoshida structural engineer Buro Happold Consulting Engineers, PC: Craig Schwitter, Amy Grahek, Sarah Kahn, Greg Otto, Sarah Sachs, Byron Stigge civil engineers Langan Engineering: George Leventis, DJ Hodson, Kostis Syngros public outreach Howard/Stein-Hudson: Arnold Bloch, Scott Giering, Christopher Ryan, Allen Zerkin economic development Economic Research Associates: Shuprotim Bhaumik, David Anderson, John Turner, Robert Wolcheski traffic engineers URS Corporation: Ira Quiat, Semyon Burshteyn, Alex Kraizman, William Lemke, William Marman, Gill Mosseri, Shawn Savage, Yixin Wang marine engineers Lawler, Matusky & Skelly Engineers LLP (LMS): Ron Alevras, Karim Abood, John Duschang

Riva-Split Waterfront
Split, Croatia, 2007
client City of Split, Croatia

architect 3LHD Architects
design team Saša Begović (Principal), Marko Dabrović (Principal), Tanja Grozdanić (Principal), Silvije Novak (Principal), Irena Mažer, Ines Avdic (Landscape) urban furniture designers Numen/ForUse: Nikola Radeljković, Sven Jonke consultants Volt-ing: M. Zanić (Electrical Planning), Nova-lux: Z. Galić i suradnici (Lighting Planning); I. Makjanić (Water and Drainage); Dr. Vladimir Andročec (Hydrology); Ivan Marušić Klif and Vjeran Salomon (Interactive Fountain and Multimedia)

High Square
Copenhagen, Denmark, 2008
client Magasin Du Nord, Realdania Fond, Copenhagen City Council architect JDS Architects (in collaboration with B.I.G.) design team Julien De Smedt (Principal, JDS Architects), Bjarke Ingels (Principal, B.I.G.), Finn Nørkjær, Henrik Juul Nielson, Jesper Wichmann, Thomas Christoffersen, Xavier Pavia Pages consultants Birch og Krogboe

Tokachi Ecology Park
Obihiro City, Japan, 2006
client Hokkaido Obihiro Civil Service and Construction office landscape architect Takano Landscape Planning Company design team Norihiro Kanekiyo (Principal), Fumiaki Takano (Principal), Yasuhiro Araki, Saido Higuchi, Etsuji Ueda, Harukazu Saito, Maki Onuki architect Atelier ZO and Pacific Consultants Inc.

Showa Kinen Park, Children's Forest
Tachikawa, Japan, 1992
client Showa Kinen Park Office, Kanto Regional Development Bureau landscape architect Takano Landscape Planning Company design team Fumiaki Takano (Principal), Norihiro Kanekiyo (Principal), Shigetoshi Aoki, Toshiko Horiuchi, Kazuko Kaneko, Yoshiko Kato, Fujiko Nakaya, Shiro Takahashi, Ogawa Tech, Taiyo Kogyo associate architect TIS Partners Co. Ltd. engineer Atsushi Kitagawara+ ILCD consultants Takano Landscape Planning Co., Ltd. (Lead Design Consultant), Fumiaki Takano (Program Manager)

A Skatepark That Glides the Land & Drops Into The Sea
San Juan, Puerto Rico, 2008
client City of San Juan, Puerto Rico architect Acconci Studio design team Vito Acconci (Principal), Dario Nuñez, Sehat Oner, Jeremy Linzee, Peter Dorsey, Sarina Basta associate architect Acconci Studio (Landscape Architect & Lighting Design) engineer Herman Diaz consultants Wormhoudt Inc. (Lead Design Consultant), PAPPR (Public Art Project of Puerto Rico), Marilu Purcell (Program Manager), Miguel Szendrey Ramos (Program Manager)

Floating Swimming Pool
Brooklyn, New York, 2006
client Ann Buttenwieser/ The Neptune Foundation, Inc. architect Jonathan Kirschenfeld Associates design team Jonathan Kirschenfeld (Principal), Stefan Danicich, Johann Mordhorst, Nicola Bormann, Andrew Woodrum naval architect CR Cushing & Co., Inc. structural engineer Robert Silman Associates, PC program manager NYC Department of Parks & Recreation construction manager Steven Sivak of SSAC lighting Tillett Lighting Design Inc. swimming pool consultant Trace Architects

Spree Bridge Bathing Ship
Berlin, Germany, 2004
client Stadtkunstprojekte e.V., Heike Catherina Müller architect (summer ship) AMP arquitectos in collaboration with Gil Wilk and Susanne Lorenz design team Felipe Artengo Rufino, Fernando Martín Menis, José Maria Rodriguez-Pastrana artist Susanne Lorenz consultants Juan Jose Gallardo (Engineer) collaborating architect (winter ship) Gil Wilk Architects with Thomas Freiwald design team Catherine von Eitzen, Thomas Freiwald, Ann-Kristin Hase, Fabian Lippert, Nora Müller, Ana Salinas, Gil Wilk consultants IB Leipold (Enclosure & Bridge), HHW + Partner (Engineer), Prof. Dr. Wagner and Prof. Dr. Gründig (Membrane Consultants)

Harbor Bath
Copenhagen, Denmark, 2003
client Copenhagen City/The Space

and Facility Foundation for Sports
architect PLOT = JDS + B.I.G.
design team Julien De Smedt (Principal, JDS Architects), Bjarke Ingels (Principal, B.I.G.), Christian Finderup, Finn Nørkjær, Henning Stuben, Ingrid Serritslev, Jakob Møller, Marc Jay consultants Birch og Krogboe

Vinaròs Urban Beach
Vinaròs, Spain, 2008
client City of Vinaròs, Ministerio de Medio Ambiente architect Guallart Architects design team Vicente Guallart (Principal), Maria Diaz associate architect Cristine Bleitcher lead design consultant Jose Miguel Iribas (Sociologist)

Urban Beaches
Paris Plage
Paris, France, 2002-

Amsterdam Plage
Amsterdam, the Netherlands, 2003-

Bruxelles Les Bains/Brussel Bad
Brussels, Belgium, 2003-

Rome Tiber Village
Rome, Italy, 2005-

Haggerston Playground
London, United Kingdom, 2005
client Haggerston Surestart architect erect architecture and Sarah Lewison design team Barbara Kaucky (Principal), Susanne Tutsch (Principal), Sarah Lewison (Artist) consultants CalDex Consultants Ltd. (Geotechnical Engineers), Stace Quantity Surveying (Quantity Surveyor)

Grounds for Play
Glasgow, United Kingdom, 2004
client Glasgow City Council and House for an Art Lover architect Gareth Hoskins Architects design team Gareth Hoskins (Principal), Joyce McCafferty engineer Glasgow City Council (Engineering, Infrastructure, and Building)

Geo Play Public Playground
Long Island City, New York, 2007
client Vernon Realty Holdings, LLC designer SonArc design team Bill Buchen (Principal), Mary Buchen (Principal) landscape architect

Ken Smith Landscape Architect architect Walker Group: Jay Valgora consultants Goldstein Associates (Structural Engineers), Kugler Associates (Lighting Designers)

Southorn Recreational Ground
Wanchai, Hong Kong, 2010
client British Council, Hong Kong architect/designer Heatherwick Studio design team Thomas Heatherwick (Principal), Ingrid Hu, Fred Manson

Westblaak Skatepark
Rotterdam, the Netherlands, 2001
client City of Rotterdam landscape architect Dirk van Peijpe (dS+V Rotterdam) design team dS+V Rotterdam: Dirk van Peijpe (Overall Design/Landscape Architect); BAR Architects: Joost Glissenaar (Staff Accommodation), Jeroen Hoorn (Small Pavilion); 75 B (Artwork: Floorpattern Design); Solos International: Jerry Beckers (Skate Objects) engineers and contractor Gemeentewerken Rotterdam

Sports Pavilion
Madrid, Spain, 2003
client Instituto Municipal de Deportes— Ayuntamiento de Madrid architect Ábalos & Herreros design team Iñaki Abalos (Principal), Juan Herreros (Principal), Renata Sentkiewicz, Angel Jaramillo, Fermina Garrido, Jakob Hense consultants Instituto Municipal de Deportes (Lead Design Consultant and Program Managers), Obiol y Moya Barcelona (Engineers)

The Garden of Knowledge
Malmö, Sweden, 2001
client Boo1 – The City of Tomorrow/ Municipality of Malmö, Sweden landscape architect Monika Gora design team Monika Gora (Principal), Caroline Kindstrand associate architect Ulf Ferrius consultants Per Johansson (Machinery Designers); Hugo Tham (Sound); Björn Nordenhake (Stonemasons); Joel Magnusson (Cultivator); Caroline Larsson, Petter Åkerblom, Gunnar Ericsson (Program Managers); Roger Johannson, Lars Molund (Timberhouse Builders)

Tentstation
Berlin, Germany, 2006
client Tentstation GbR: Sarah Oßwald, Jessica Zeller, Petr Barth, Bernd Häußler architect büro für planung + raum/berlin design team Petr Barth (Principal), Bernd Häußler (Principal) consultant Weistplan Berlin (Contractor)

Balham Community Space
London, United Kingdom, 2005
client Artmarkit architect Lynch Architects design team Patrick Lynch (Principal), Naomi Shaw (Associate Architect), Jacques Dahan collaborators Elliott Wood (Engineer), Sainsbury's & Wandsworth Council (Program Managers) contractor RG Group

Metropolitan Park
Rio de Janeiro, Brazil, 2005
client Municipality of Rio de Janeiro architect Jorge Mario Jáuregui design team Jorge Mario Jáuregui (Principal), Cristian Sigulin, Fernando Newlands, Sylvain Hérbert, Jean Baptiste Fourmont, Carolina Dardi consultants Pedro Aleixo (Management of Physical-Territorial Survey), Marilena Giacomini (Management of Social-Economical Survey), Fernando Newlands (Management of Institutional Survey), Carlos Montano (Environmental Consultant), David Cardeman (Urban Legislation Consultant), Milton Feferman (Housing Consultant), Aldo Rosa (Geotechnical Consultant), Cleumo Cordoville (Urban Infrastructure Consultant), Ricardo Esteves (Transport Consultant)

Floating Park
Seoul, Korea, 2007
client Sungbuk District Office in Seoul architect IROJE KHM architects & planners design team Hyo Man Kim (Principal), Jung Min Oh, A Rum Kim, Sun Hee Kim associate architect Su Mi Jeong consultants MOA & Consulting Engineers, Ltd. (Structure Designers) Litework (Lighting Designers)

The High Line
New York, New York, 2008
client team NYC Department of Parks & Recreation, NYC Economic Development Corporation, Office of the Deputy Mayor for Economic Development and Rebuilding, NYC Department of City Planning, Friends of the High Line architects Field Operations and Diller Scofidio + Renfro design team Field Operations (Landscape Architecture/Urban Design): James Corner (Principal), Tom Jost, Lisa Switkin, Nahyun Hwang, Maura Rockcastle; Diller Scofidio + Renfro (Architecture): Ric Scofidio (Principal), Elizabeth Diller (Principal), Charles Renfro (Principal), Matthew Johnson, Tobias Hegemann, Gaspar Libedinsky; Piet Oudolf (Planting Design): Piet Oudolf; L'Observatoire International (Lighting Design): Herves Descottes, Annette Goderbauer, Jeff Beck; Pentagram Design, Inc. (Signage): Paula Scher, Rion Byrd, Andrew Freeman, Jennifer Rittner; VJ Associates (Capital & Operating Cost Estimating): Vijay Desai, Sushma Tammareddi, Chongba Sherpa; ETM Associates (Public Space Management): Tim Marshall; Ducibella Venter & Santor (Security & Operating Consultants): Robert Ducibella, Michael Hughes; Barker Mohandas (Vertical Transport Consultants): Rick Barker, Paul Bennett; Northern Designs (Irrigation Consultants and Designers): Michael Astram; Control Point Associates, Inc. (Site Surveyor): Paul Jurkowski; Applied Ecological Services (Ecology): Mark O'Leary engineers Buro Happold (Structural/ MEP Engineering): Craig Schwitter, Mark Dawson, Dennis Burton, Andrew Coats, Anthony Curiale, Beth Macri, Sean O'Neill; Robert Silman Associates (Structural Engineering/Historic Preservation): Joseph Tortorella, Andre Georges; GRB Services, Inc (Environmental Engineering/Site Remediation): Richard Barbour, Steven Panter, Rose Russo; Philip Habib & Associates (Civil & Traffic Engineering/ Zoning & Landuse): Philip Habib, Sandy Pae; Code Consultants Professional Engineers (Code Consultants): John McCormick, Laurence Dallaire

Oakland Waterfront Trail
Oakland, California, 2007
client City of Oakland, Office of Public Works designers Hood Design, EDAW, and Murakami Nelson consultants Moffatt & Nichol,

Wallace Roberts & Todd, Inc., Johansing Iron Works

Can You See Me Now?
Worldwide, 2001-
artists Blast Theory in collaboration with the Mixed Reality Lab, University of Nottingham

99 Red Balloons
San José, California, 2006
client ISEA/ZeroOne: A Global Festival of Art on the Edge artists Jenny Marketou and Katie Salen

Karaoke Ice
San José, California, 2006
clients ZeroOne San Jose, San Jose State University, Lucas Artists Program at Montalvo artists Nancy Nowacek, Katie Salen, and Marina Zurkow

Power Station London
London, United Kingdom, 2010
client Parkview International architect ATOPIA design team Jane Harrison (Principal), David Turnbull (Principal), Azra Aksamija, Babak Bryan, Jeg Dudley lead design consultant and engineer ARUP program manager Bovis Lend Lease Parkview International

PITCH: Juba
Juba, Southern Sudan, 2007
strategic partners UNICEF, ECHO architect ATOPIA research design team Jane Harrison (Principal) David Turnbull (Principal), Peter Albertson, Aimee Chang engineers ARUP Water: Ian Carradice; King Shaw: Doug King; SIEMENS Roke Manor: Mike Hook supporters PAT-Forage International: Adam Ashforth; Barcode Logistics FZCO/JUBA

Pillow Fight Union Square
New York, New York, 2006
group Newmindspace artists Kevin Bracken, Lori Cherilyn Kufner

London Roof
London, United Kingdom, 2002
group Office of Subversive Architecture design team Karsten Huneck, Bernd Truempler consultants Johannes Marburg (Photography Consultant), Tamara Hall (Text Consultant)

Parkour
Worldwide, 1985-
founder David Belle

Yellow Arrow Projects
Worldwide, 2004-
group Counts Media

Electronic Lens (e-Lens)
Manresa, Spain, 2006
client MIT, Direcció d'Atenció Ciutadana de la Generalitat de Catalunya, Ajuntament de Manresa group MIT Media Lab project directors William J. Mitchell, Federico Casalegno course collaborator Jonathan Gips MIT workshop students Aaron Zinman, Allison Novak, Anne Dodge, Enrico Costanza, Gena Peditto, Jae-woo Chung, Jie-Eun Hwang, Miguel Menchu Luarte, Mirja Leinss, Ommed Sathe, Retro Poblano, Sajid Sadi, Stephanie Groll, Tad Hirsch, Vanessa Bertozzi, Wooyoung Kimm website Caitlin Winner

P2P: Power to the People
Kitchener, Canada, 2002
Toronto, Canada, 2004
San José, California, 2006
artist Gorbet Design design team Matt Gorbet, Susan Gorbet, Rob Gorbet

Inbetween
London, United Kingdom, 2005
architect erect architecture design team Barbara Kaucky (Principal), Susanne Tutsch (Principal) funder HCVS, Neighbourhood Renewal Unit

News.Box.Walk
New York, New York, 2004
artist Christina Ray (Glowlab)

Santa Fe Railyard Park
Santa Fe, New Mexico, 2007
client The Trust for Public Land: Brian Drypolcher landscape architect Ken Smith Landscape Architect, Mary Miss, and Frederic Schwartz Architects design team Ken Smith Landscape Architect: Ken Smith (Principal), Alex Felson (Project Manager), Joseph Herda (Project Manager), Matt Landis (Project Manager), Elizabeth Asawa, David Hamerman, Daniel Willner, Judith Wong, Yuka Yoshida; Mary

Miss Studio: Mary Miss; Frederic Schwartz Architects: Frederic Schwartz (Principal), Julia Murphy, Douglas Romines consultants Harris Consultants: Brett Harris, Mike Harris, Eduardo Ramirez; URS Corporation: Robert Bookwalter, Anthony Naranjo; Laboratory of Landscape Architecture: Edith Katz; Jim Conti Lighting Design: Jim Conti; Dan Euser Water Architecture: Dan Euser; Wallace Laboratories: Garn Wallace; Gayla Bechtol Architect: Gayla Bechtol; Regenesis: Joel Glanzberg; Earthwright Designs: Richard Jennings; Watershed West: Richard Jennings; Balis & Company: Jon Balis

River Coast Park
Buenos Aires, Argentina, 2001
client Municipality of Vicente López (Mayor Enrique García) architect Arch. Claudio Vekstein design team Claudio Vekstein (Principal), Georg Ponzelar, Luis Etchegorry, Andreas Lengfeld, Eugenia Frías Moreno, Jonas Norsted, Franco Neira, Santiago Mendibour, Alejandro Goldemberg, Enterprise Foundation of Vicente López (Pres. José Menoyo) consultants Marcelo Rufino Assoc.: Tomás del Carril and Fontán Balestra (Structural Engineers), Lucia Schiappapietra (Landscape Architecture), Claudio Vekstein (Lighting Designer) construction management Claudio Vekstein (Monument), Municipality of Vicente López, Public Works and Planning Departments (Coast Park & Amphitheater) contractor SAPIC S.A. Constructions, Ing. Roberto Van den Broek (Monument and Amphitheater), Municipality of Vicente López (Coast Park)

Post-Industrial Park
Eberswalde, Germany, 2002
client Landesgartenschau Eberswalde 2002 GmbH architect Topotek1 design team Martin Rein-Cano (Principal), Lorenz Dexler (Principal), Andreas Kicherer, Frank Feinle, Rita Mettler, Sebastian Hauser, Marion v. Kutschenbach, Hagen Lorenz, Janna de Haen, Inga Hahn, Dan Budik, Janina Fitermann, George Mahnke, Björn Krack, Jörg Sieweke, Frank Pötzl, Andreas Westendorf consultants Isterling & Partner, ARGE LaGa2002

Eberswalde, Regioplan Eberswalde,
IBE Eberswalde + Büro Diehme
Eberswalde

Dania Park
Malmö, Sweden, 2002
client City of Malmö, Sweden
landscape architect Thorbjörn
Andersson and PeGe Hillinge design
team Thorbjörn Andersson (Principal),
PeGe Hillinge (Principal), Veronika
Borg, Peter Ekrot, Clotte Frank, Anders
Lidström lighting designer Michael
Hallbert consultants VBB structural
engineers contractor Skanska Ltd

Park and Jog
Manchester, United Kingdom, 1999
client Salford University/Royal
Institute of British Architects
(Competition's Office) architect
Buschow Henley design team Ralph
Buschow (Principal), Gavin Hale-
Brown (Principal), Simon Henley
(Principal), Ken Rorrison (Principal),
Suzannah Waldron, Claire Johnson,
Josephine Larsen

Olympic Sculpture Park
Seattle, Washington, 2006
client Seattle Art Museum architecture
and site design Weiss/Manfredi design
team Marion Weiss and Michael A.
Manfredi (Design Partners), Christopher
Ballentine (Project Manager), Todd
Hoehn (Project Architect), Yehre Suh
(Project Architect), Michael Blasberg,
Emily Clanahan, Lauren Crahan, Kok
Kian Goh, Hamilton Hadden, Mike
Harshman, Mustapha Jundi, Justin
Kwok, John Peek, Akari Takebayashi
consultants Magnusson Klemenic
Associates (Structural and Civil
Engineering Consultant), Charles
Anderson Landscape Architecture
(Landscape Architecture Consultant),
Owen Richards Architects (Art Program
Coordinator), ABACUS Engineered
Systems (Mechanical and Electrical
Engineering Consultant), Brandston
Partnership Inc. (Lighting Design
Consultant), Hart Crowser (Geotech-
nical Engineering Consultant), Aspect
Consulting (Environmental Consultant),
Anchor Environmental (Aquatic
Engineering Consultant), Pentagram
(Graphics Consultant), ARUP (Security
and AV/IT Consultant), Barrientos LLC
(Project Management)

Northern Park
Amsterdam, the Netherlands, 2010
client Stadsdeel Amsterdam Noord
landscape architect West 8 Urban
Design and Landscape Architecture
design team Adriaan Geuze (Principal),
Theo Reesink, Riëtte Bosch, Ard
Middeldorp, Karsten Buchholz, Jacco
Stuy, Cyrus Clark, Jonas Vanneste
associate architect ABT Arhhem
(Engineer) consultants Stadsdeel
Amsterdam Noord (Program Managers)

Velo-City
Toronto, Canada, 2004
architect Chris Hardwicke

image credits

Van Alen Institute thanks the following individuals and firms for generously granting permission to reproduce their materials in The Good Life *exhibition and catalogue.*

p. 22
Idea Store Whitechapel
1: Lyndon Douglas
2, 3, 4, 5: Tim Soar

p. 23
Denia Mountain Project
1, 2, 3, 4: Guallart Architects

p. 24
SOMOHO
1, 2, 3: Katy Marks

p. 25
Stadium Culture
1: Jovanovic Weiss & NAO

Eib's Pond Park Outdoor Classroom
1, 2: Mark LaRocca

p. 26
Biblioteca degli Alberi
1, 2, 3: Inside Outside

p. 27
Heerlijkheid Hoogvliet
1, 2, 3: FAT

p. 28
Homerton Struggle Niche
1, 2: Nils Norman

Alexanderplatz
1: RACA

p. 29
PARK(ing)
1, 2: Andrea Scher

Guerilla Gardeners
1: Erin Wood

GuerrillaGardening.org
2: Richard Reynolds

p. 30
Coventry Phoenix Initiative
1: Jochen Gerz
2: Marc Goodwin
3: Michael Rummey/Rummey Design Associates

p. 31
Public Art Projects
1: Greyworld

Solkan Fountain
1: Sadar Vuga Arhitekti

Park Bench House
1: Hayley Franklin

p. 32
Römerkastell and Marktplatz
1: Nimbus GmbH

Public Art Projects
1: T. Heys-Cerchio

Jumping Field
1: Kuvataiteen keskusarkisto, Pirje Mykkänen

p. 38-39
Contemporary Music Center
1, 2, 3, 4, 5: Stan Allen Architects

p. 40-41
Flux Park, King's Cross
1, 2, 3, 4, 5: General Public Agency

p. 42
North Plaza, Lincoln Center for the Performing Arts
1, 2, 3, 4: Diller Scofidio + Renfro

p. 43
Barking Town Square
1, 2, 3: muf architecture/art

p. 44-45
Grand Canal Square
1, 2: Hayes Davidson, courtesy of the Dublin Docklands Development Authority
3: Martha Schwartz, Inc.

p. 46-47
East River Waterfront Study
1, 2, 3, 4, 5, 6: SHoP Architects, Richard Rogers Partnership, Ken Smith Landscape Architect

p. 48
Riva-Split Waterfront
1, 2, 3, 4, 5: 3LHD Architects

p. 54-55
High Square
1, 2, 3, 4, 5, 6: JDS Architects (in collaboration with B.I.G.)

p. 56-57
Tokachi Ecology Park
1, 4: Chikato Kyoya
2, 3, 5: Takano Landscape Planning Co., Ltd.

p. 58
Skatepark
1, 2, 3, 4: Acconci Studio

p. 59
Floating Swimming Pool

1: Karl Jensen/ Jonathan Kirschenfeld Associates
2: Jonathan Kirschenfeld Associates

Spree Bridge Bathing Ship
1: Courtesy Gil Wilk
2: Kulturarena Veranstaltungs GmbH

p. 60
Harbor Bath
1: Julien De Smedt

Vinaròs Urban Beach
1: Guallart Architects

p. 61
Urban Beaches
1: Mairie de Paris
2: Silvia Poggioli
3: Barbara Hartman
4: Jean-Loup Vandewiele— Brussels City

p. 62
Haggerston Playground
1: David Grandorge

Grounds for Play
1: Glasgow City Council and Gareth Hoskins Architects

Geo Play Public Playground
1: Ken Smith Landscape Architect, Bill and Mary Buchen/SonArc, Inc.

p. 63
Southorn Recreational Ground
1, 2, 3: Heatherwick Studio

Westblaak Skatepark
1: Dirk van Peijpe

Sports Pavilion
1: Bleda y Rosa

p. 64
The Garden of Knowledge
1, 2, 3: Urszula Striner

Tentstation
1: Courtesy Sarah Oßwald, Jessica Zeller, Petr Barth, Bernd Häußler

Balham Community Space
1: N. Tracey

p. 70
Metropolitan Park

1: Jorge Mario Jáuregui
2, 3: Gabriel Leandro Jáuregui
4: Jorge Mario Jáuregui

p. 71
Floating Park
1, 2, 3: IROJE KHM architects & planners

p. 72-73
The High Line
1, 2, 3, 4: Field Operations and Diller Scofidio + Renfro, Courtesy The City of New York

p. 74
Oakland Waterfront Trail
1, 2: Hood Design

p. 75
Can You See Me Now?
1: Blast Theory

99 Red Balloons
1, 2: Jenny Marketou and Katie Salen

Karaoke Ice
3: Nancy Nowacek, Katie Salen, and Marina Zurkow

p. 76
Power Station London
1, 2, 3: ATOPIA

p. 77
PITCH: Juba
1, 2, 3: ATOPIA research

p. 78
Pillow Fight Union Square
1: http://whatisee.org

London Roof
2: Johannes Marburg

Parkour
1, 2: Andy Day, Kiell.com urbanfreeflow.com

p. 79
Yellow Arrow Projects
1: Michael Counts
2: Nathan Phillips

Electronic Lens (e-Lens)
1, 2: Mirja Leinss

P2P: Power to the People
1, 2: Gorbet Design, Inc.

p. 80
Inbetween
1: erect architecture
2, 3: Herman Djoumessi

News.Box.Walk
1, 2: Christina Ray

p. 86-87
Santa Fe Railyard Park
1, 2, 3, 4: Ken Smith Landscape Architect

p. 88
River Coast Park
1: Claudio Vekstein
2: Sergio Esmoris
3: Michelo Guzzo
4: Claudio Vekstein
5: MVL

p. 89
Post-Industrial Park
1, 2, 3, 4, 5: Hanns Joosten

p. 90
Dania Park
1: Thorbjörn Andersson
2, 3: Lennart Pettersson

p. 91
Park and Jog
1, 2, 3: Buschow Henley

p. 92-93
Olympic Sculpture Park, Seattle Art Museum
1, 2, 3, 4, 5, 6: Weiss/Manfredi

p. 94-95
Northern Park
1, 2, 3, 4, 5, 6, 7, 8: West 8

p. 96
Velo-City
1, 2, 3, 4: Chris Hardwicke

exhibition credits

Curator
Zoë Ryan

Exhibition Design and Installation
WORK Architecture Company—
Amale Andraos
Dan Wood
Skye Beach
Olaf Haertel
Forrest Jessee
Anna Kenoff
Ryan Neiheiser
Dayoung Shin
Linda Choe Vestergaard
Elastico/Elodie Blanchard
(Fabric consulting and design)
Eze Bongo (Construction consulting)

Exhibition Graphic Design
Project Projects—
Prem Krishnamurthy
Adam Michaels
Caroline Askew
Chris McCaddon
Ken Meier
Local Projects (Media consulting)

Motion Graphics
Project Projects with
Local Projects
Craig Cook (Video production)

Exhibition Committee
Adi Shamir, VAI Executive Director
Sherida E. Paulsen, VAI Chair
Paola Antonelli, VAI Trustee
Susan T. Rodriguez, VAI Trustee

The Public Space Roundtables
Janet Abrams, Paola Antonelli,
Benjamin Aranda, Diana Balmori,
Donald Bates, Adrian Benepe,
Michael Bierut, Andrew Darrell,
Jonathan Evans, Carl Goodman,
DeeDee Gordon, Jane Harrison,
Mark Husser, Natalie Jeremijenko,
Steven Johnson, Arnold Lehman,
Jeanne Lutfy, Gregg Pasquarelli,
Anne Pasternak, Charles Renfro,
Susan T. Rodriguez, Katie Salen,
Craig Schwitter, Kevin Slavin,
Ken Smith, Cliff Sperber, Dana
Spiegel, Paul Stoller, Marilyn Taylor,
Marc Tsurumaki, Camille Utterback,
Andrew C. Winters, Dan Wood

VAI Exhibition Team
Karen Kice, Research Assistant
Elise Youn, Curatorial Assistant
Jonah Lowenfeld, Copyeditor
Uriah Leddy, Videographer (Interviews)
Jamie Hand
Ori Topaz
Marcus Woollen
Chun Ouyang
Carolyn Acevedo
Isaac H. Margulis
Ari Duraku

Urban Game Design and Development
area/code—
Frank Lantz (Design and creative lead)
Kevin Slavin (Design and creative lead)
Wilson Chang
Kati London
Chris Paretti
Scott Jon Siegel
Erik Högstedt (Lead technical development/consulting)
Dennis Crowley (Technical development/consulting)
Michael Sharon (Technical development/consulting)
Dan Melinger (Technical development/consulting)

Sponsors
The Good Life exhibition—
National Endowment for the Arts
Graham Foundation for
      Advanced Studies in the Fine Arts
New York State Council on the Arts
Con Edison
Brightman Hill Charitable Foundation
Diane von Furstenberg
Josh Weisberg/Scharff Weisberg Inc.
Look-Look
Restaurant Florent
Material for the Arts
2(x)ist

Special thanks to
Hudson River Park Trust

The Good Life catalogue—
The Stephen A. and Diana L.
      Goldberg Foundation
Elise Jaffe + Jeffrey Brown

Van Alen Institute

Van Alen Institute: Projects in Public Architecture is an internationally recognized generator and platform for new ideas and initiatives for improving the design of the public realm. Since it began its program of Projects in Public Architecture in the fall of 1995, the Institute has directed exhibitions, design studies and competitions, lectures, conferences, and publications designed to research and communicate the critical role of design in regenerating cities. While the Institute's projects are grounded in the challenges and opportunities in New York, the projects are structured to engage an interdisciplinary and state, nation, and worldwide array of practitioners, policymakers, students, educators, and civic leaders. Each project, from an ideas competition for Governors Island in 1996 to major exhibitions, such as *OPEN: New Designs for Public Space* in 2003 and *The Good Life: New Public Spaces For Recreation* in 2006, is designed to be a catalyst for changing perceptions and possibilities for the future of public life.

Model of *The Good Life* exhibition on Hudson River Park's Pier 40, New York, New York
Model: WORKac

Hudson River Park's Pier 40 with exterior graphics
Rendering: Project Projects

Published by
Van Alen Institute
30 W 22 Street, 6th Floor
New York, NY 10010
Tel +1 (212) 924-7000
Fax +1 (212) 366-5836
www.vanalen.org

Editor
Zoë Ryan

Design
Project Projects

Typeface
Bryant 2 Pro Medium
Process Type Foundry

Printing and Binding
Kromar

Distributed by
Princeton Architectural Press
37 East 7th Street
New York, NY 10003
Tel +1 (800) 722-6657
www.papress.com

ISBN: 1-56898-628-9
ISBN: 978-1-56898-628-9

Library of Congress Cataloging-in-Publication Data
is available from the publisher.